# SEEING
# THROUGH
# THE MEDIA

# SEEING THROUGH THE MEDIA

## A Religious View of Communication and Cultural Analysis

MICHAEL WARREN

TRINITY PRESS INTERNATIONAL
Harrisburg, Pennsylvania

First Paperback Edition 1997

Trinity Press International, P.O. Box 1321, Harrisburg, PA 17105
Trinity Press International is a division of the Morehouse Group

**Library of Congress Cataloging-in-Publication Data**
Warren, Michael, 1935-
    [Communications and cultural analysis]
    Seeing through the media : a religious view of communications and cultural analysis / by Michael Warren.
        p.   cm.
    Originally published: Westport, Conn. : Bergin & Garvey, 1992.
    Includes bibliographical references and index.
    ISBN 1-56338-211-3 (pbk. : alk. paper)
    1. Popular culture – Religious aspects.  2. Popular culture – United States.  3. Religion and culture – United States.  4. Communication – Religious aspects.  5. United States – Religion – 1960-     I. Title.
    BL2525.W39   1997
    291.1′7–dc21                                                      97-27068
                                                                            CIP

Printed in the United States of America

97    98    99    00    01    02        6    5    4    3    2    1

*For James Reese, OSFS (1926–1989),*
*a priest, scholar, peacemaker,*
*justice-seeker, and colleague*
*— whose life merits imitation.*

# CONTENTS

# ACKNOWLEDGMENTS

I, myself, wrote this book but not by myself. In the background is a group of persons who offered various kinds of assistance without which it would never have been written, let alone published. This assistance included encouragement, a sounding board for ideas, reactions to various drafts, suggestions for revisions, and sometimes, hard questions. They all took the time to read and comment, even when they did not have the time. Here, prior to any others, I thank Connie Loos for encouraging me to even consider this project and for being present to it throughout by reading and advice. But there are others I wish publicly to name, acknowledging and offering thanks for their help.

Jim Reese, a colleague in the Department of Theology and Religious Studies at St. John's, read the earliest draft of this work, three incomplete chapters seeking a clear focus, and from his fine background in semiotics, marked up almost every page with suggestions and questions. If he had not encouraged me to continue at that point, I would probably have given up. This book, whose completion he did not live to see, is for him. Others who helped in differing but important ways include, first, Connie Loos, and then Paul Medici, Dean of St. John's Graduate School of Arts and Sciences, Dwayne Huebner, Gregory Baum, Phil and Liz Marinelli, Brian Donahue-Lynch, Michael-Paul Gallagher, SJ, Martin Kennedy and Breda Brady, Colette McCarthy, Paula Goggin, Jim Briglia, Graham Rossiter, Don Kraus, Bob Browning, Anthony Fasano, and John Kavanaugh, SJ.

While the first edition of this book would not have been published without the connections forged by Marianne Sawicki out of her special interdisciplinary scholarship, the second edition was made possible by persons, most of whom I have never met, who gave careful reviews to a book not fitting the usual categories. They include Jim DiGiacomo, SJ, Mark Francis, CSV, Jeff Astley, Chris Arthur, Kathryn Tanner, and George Brown. Deserving special mention is Ed Farley, who thoughtfully directed me to Trinity Press International.

Most of us cannot sing without a chorus nor write books without help. These persons were my help and to them I say thanks. A special category of help came from Frances Fico of St. John's University, secretary to the Philosophy and Theology Departments, for her patient printing and duplicating of various drafts, for the index and bibliography, and for seeing through various complex tasks involving computers. To her, special thanks.

The three-and-a-half-year period of writing this book was not only spread out in unanticipated ways but very much enriched by the arrival of two children, Catherine and Justin. Seeing culture through a child's eyes is something only they could have added to this book.

# INTRODUCTION

The studies that eventually led to this book were done in 1984–85, during a sabbatical year of study. Having come to the conclusion that the most powerful educative channels had long since passed from the hands of those who called themselves educators, and reacting against what I considered to be the exaggerated claims of religious educators, I decided to study the question of influences from its broadest angle, that of culture. My problem was where to begin. I had done some limited reading on culture, but none of it helped me answer my own questions. It did not give me a fundamental way of thinking about culture that related it to the concrete situations of everyday life.

Possibly because of my own background in the sociology of religion, I was drawn to Raymond Williams's writings, which looked at culture more through a sociological lens than an anthropological one. Starting with Williams's *The Sociology of Culture,* I worked my way backwards and forwards through his many writings. Williams answered many of my questions and opened me to a new way of thinking about reality. Still, for every question answered, new ones opened up. It was as if I had found an artist to inspire me but had yet to let that inspiration influence my own artistic practice. I myself needed to find a more systematic way by which I could apply the principles by which culture could be seen and then evaluated. From among the methods for dealing with these questions, could I work one out for myself? If I succeeded, would it then be possible to present this method in language accessible to others, such as secular educators, theologians, religious educators, religious practitioners, including parents? In my mind I kept coming back

1

to a model for such a presentation of method, namely, the simple one Joe Holland and Peter Henriot had outlined in their 1980 work, *Social Analysis: Linking Faith with Justice*. Their booklet gave a general but educated audience access to a rudimentary kind of social analysis. What might a rudimentary kind of cultural analysis look like?

And so this book began as a way of talking to myself, of pushing further against my own questions. Every bit of it was written as an exercise in learning to speak, in a search for a language to describe a relatively new problem in a new age of electronic communications. It was my own attempt at cultural agency. The process was intimidating, like fishing with a drop line from a dingy dangerously drifting toward the open sea. These waters were new to me, and regularly I had a sense of being out of my depth. How far or how deep dare I go without losing sight of the shore? Like anyone not trained for uncharted waters, I preferred the guidance of clear maps and felt lost without one.

One of my biggest problems in the writing of these chapters was finding persons interested enough in what I was trying to do to read drafts of what in the beginning was dense, tedious prose. Gradually I found readers, mostly former students and friends, willing as a favor to review what I wrote and tell me candidly what they thought. Named in the acknowledgments, they represent the sort of cross-section of interests from which I hope to draw any readership for this book.

Though the study began in 1984, I was ready to begin writing this book only in early January 1988 and did not finish until May 1991. This was by far the most difficult writing project I have attempted. Everything I published during that period — two dozen essays and two books (*Youth, Gospel, Liberation* [1987] and *Faith, Culture, and the Worshiping Community* [1989]) — was heavily influenced by my study of culture. In a very real way, I was trying to translate my own reading into categories accessible to a variety of other persons, from ordinary religious adherents to professors. When these essays and books began to appear, people beyond my circle of friends and colleagues indicated that I was dealing with their questions too, and not just my own. From such responses came the courage to keep working on this book.

As it turned out, during these years culture came to be *the* intellectual issue of the day, something it promises to be for some time into the future. Whose curriculum is worthy of study? Whose voices are being heard, whose ignored? How can we recover the lost voices of history? How can cultural imperialism be overturned? Those on the Right and the Left have now come to see deep issues of power latent in cultural assumptions, with the Right in general becoming more and more alarmed at having their long-secure assumptions questioned. Indeed, an understanding of culture has important political implications. In this climate, the churches, synagogues, and other religious groups have only begun to probe culture's implications for their members. Meanwhile, the colonization of the attention of ordinary persons progresses exponentially.

My hope is that this book will be of help to those who sense the centrality of these issues for our time. For some it will be an introduction to the thought of Raymond Williams. For others, it will offer, I hope, a way of thinking about cultural production that will help them in their profession as educators. For still others, those with religious commitments, I hope this book discloses how decisive the matter of culture is for religious communities. Though it may at first sound "grand" to say it, I know of no other single book that seeks to do what this one does: to foster a new sense of our ability to talk back to the meanings and signs presented for our consumption and to lay the groundwork of a method for doing so. That means this book is a beginning.

I have been so acutely aware of its shortcomings that, as a way of staying with it, I had to keep reminding myself I was writing it primarily for myself. *I* needed to write it, even were it never published. By working on small sections, being satisfied to talk to myself about such and such an aspect of the project, I was able to keep on going. These sections had to be revised over and over again, some re-written six and seven times before they said what I wanted them to say. In this way the project grew. What initially I thought might be three chapters of a booklet became in the end the seven chapters found here.

And so, since this book, written in such a tentative process, is a beginning, I invite any and all to critique and question, to affirm and/or rebut, and to push against the ideas found here. Only in this way will any of us progress in the task of talking back to culture. If in five years there are many more works on cultural analysis, most of them revealing the meagerness of this one, my work will have been well-rewarded.

I encourage readers to use this book in the light of their own interests, as a kind of handbook to be mined for information or skills they find helpful. Which of the ways of approaching culture and communications are helpful? Are there skills here that can be taught others? Some may find the historical sections unnecessarily complicated for their current interests and should be free to skip them, temporarily or permanently, to get on to the more "practical" sections. Others will find the historical and theoretical material essential but will want to skim over the specific allusions to concrete situations. Since this book was written out of my own interests, I invite readers to look to their own questions and intuitions in reading it.

Before readers plunge into the pages that follow, two matters need to be highlighted. One has to do with the word "religious" in my title and especially in the body of the book. The second has to do with the issue of censorship.

The word "religious" is a general term, but the phenomenon of being religious is specific. One becomes religious in specifically committed patterns of life lived in specific communities. I intend this book for persons of any religious background — Jewish, Christian, Muslim, Hindu, Buddhist, etc. — because the problems posed by electronic communications affect them all. Any place where I use the term "religious," I am consciously intending the idea as applicable to any religious tradition. However, since religiousness is also specific, I found that I had to use examples of how various issues might affect a particular tradition. Had I worked hard enough at it, I probably could have found specific examples tied to every major religion. However, in the end I decided to use the examples I knew from my own religious background: the Roman Church in the Christian tradition. My hope is that these specifically Roman Catholic examples will not become barriers to readers in finding the analogous examples in their own traditions. Poetry suggests that the most specific is also potentially the most universal, something I hope will prove true for readers.

Often in these pages I recommend the centrality of judgment in cultural agency. Judgment evaluates quality or its lack, humanizing vision or its lack. Some will ask if I am advocating censorship, which obstructs cultural production deemed dangerous or unhealthy. My basic answer is: No. Nowhere here do I advocate censorship. Everywhere I advocate judgment and action based on judgment. I encourage groups of any size to lay out their evaluation of signification: either positive or negative, and to make it public. The process can help sharpen judgment. If their judgment is negative, they can encourage or even organize protest or boycott. This is judgment in action, not censorship.

However, I must admit that daily I see examples of carefully produced "stuff" — songs, advertisements, TV, and filmed material — that the world might, in my view, be better off without. I might even be tempted to think I would censor this or that particular item if I could. But when I consider the various groups hot to censor and some of the works of art they would have censored had they been able to, I keep coming back to the importance of protecting freedom of expression. I have made up my mind but not in a definitive way.

Feminists with impeccable credentials on civil liberties keep alive for me this question of what should be allowable in society. Is there a point, for instance, where depictions of the brutalization of women endanger all women? If so, should these depictions be tolerated? Catharine MacKinnon and Andrea Dworkin, to mention two, have brought this question to the fore. In the course of this book I ask whether we might extend to advertisements aimed at children — or to other kinds of cultural products — consumer-protection rules which now apply to manufactured products such as children's toys. And so, I say no to censorship while continuing to reflect on this issue from various angles.[1]

If the censorship issue is raised in the minds of readers, they will also find a host of other matters raised, again, without offering definitive solutions. This is as it should be. This book is a beginning, meant to spark thinking, not to close it off.

## NOTES

1. A perceptive but concise treatment of underlying issues is Ronald Dworkin, "Liberty and Pornography," *New York Review of Books* 38, no. 14 (15 August 1991): 12–15.

*Chapter 1*

# THE PROBLEM OF POPULAR CULTURE

## How I Came to Write This Book

This book comes from my years of work as an educator and catechist. Though, as will become clear, it is not about young people, it had its beginnings in my often vague reflections arising from work with young people and from trying to understand the influences in their lives. As a high school teacher, then as a parish catechist, and now as a university professor, I have been preoccupied with what young people paid attention to and why. Seeking to influence others toward religious understanding and insight, I saw religious tradition function as only one among many influences, and in many cases, a weak one.

Early on as a high school teacher, I realized that the school, for all the important goals it set out for itself, was not the major influence it wished to be and had perhaps overstated its role. Years later I came across Henri Marrou's description of the limited role expected of schools in antiquity because of the major role the wider culture was expected to have in education:

> [At this time, third century and later,] schools did not play the all-important part in education which they were to play in the Middle Ages. The schoolmaster was only responsible for one small section of children's education — the mental side. He did not really educate his pupils. Education means, essentially, moral training,

7

character training, a whole way of life. The "master" was only expected to teach them to read — which is a much less important matter.[1]

Many of the young people I have known held notions about school similar to those of the third century: School is not a whole way of life. What caught their attention more fully were matters beyond the school: music, the heroes being proposed to them, fashion, films and TV, patterns of work, of leisure, of using money.

If I as a teacher wanted to have their attention — and I judged that disciplined learning demanded focused attention — I needed to know more about these other matters: what they were, what their significance was, and how that significance emerged. Teaching the possibilities of peacemaking, for example, was difficult when film and television glorified the acts of war-waging. So too, if the church wanted to be a zone of influence among young people, it could only do so by examining carefully and thinking wisely about these other influences. My later work with adults convinced me that similar patterns of work, leisure, and use of money were also the main influences shaping their attention.

In examining young people's heroes, fashion, music, film, and TV, I saw how fully these media engaged their imaginations. Within the past sixty years or so, with the development of radio, film, and then television, graphic depictions of "how things are" have become both increasingly accessible to all and increasingly vivid. These developments changed not only the means by which reality could be imagined; they made the imagination of reality itself more tangible and vivid. The way an imagination of life is communicated has shifted dramatically — and I use this adverb in its literal sense. Media analyst George Gerbner puts the change this way:

We have moved away from the historic experience of humankind. Children used to grow up in a home where parents told most of the stories. Today television tells most of the stories to most of the people most of the time.[2]

These stories tend to have a taken-for-granted quality to them; people see them but in general are unable to think about how they see them. During the teen years, young people try on various "imaginations" of themselves in an effort to find one that fits. These imaginations are part of a broader project in young people's lives: they are trying to imagine the kind of person they wish to be, what their future life will be like, and the kind of person they wish to share it with. If the process of establishing an identity is, in part, a process of imagining for oneself possible forms of behavior, possible attitudes and values, possible goals, and ultimately, a possible future, then those who propose these imagined possibilities wield special influence.

"Those who propose these imagined possibilities." In these words lie easily overlooked but important aspects of the way influence works in our world. Human hands are involved in producing the imaginations proposed to the young. The dreams of the young do not just "happen" but are planned and produced by particular persons, usually working in tandem with groups of other persons. "Orchestrate" may be the most accurate English word to describe the efforts of these persons working to influence the young. Seen this way, the proposal to youth of various ways of imagining the possibilities of life is not accidental or mysterious. The proposals and the processes by which they are produced and communicated can be identified and examined. They are open to scrutiny if only we will allow ourselves to pay attention to them.

Though I use the word "orchestrate," I am not describing here a conspiracy but rather the way initiatives can come together and coalesce. The specific imaginations are planned, produced, and communicated, but the precise way they come together to create an overall sense of reality may not have been planned by any single person or group. An ad-maker presents, as part of overall proposal of the ad, the young male as a warrior. Such an imagination of young men works with similar depictions in film, TV, and music to make such an imagination seem natural. Overlooking such processes, some prefer to ascribe imaginations of the self to psychological processes, arising from the conflicts and dynamisms within the person and the person's emotive environment. Though one's vulnerability to certain imaginations of the self may indeed be based in the psyche, the actual production of various imaginations is less a psychological than a social reality, the end result of networks of persons and agencies seeking to imagine the world for the young.

Put this way, the influences on the young are neither inevitable or inexplicable. Whatever their complexities, they are social products whose production can be studied. From this angle, influences operating through media such as film, radio, television, advertising, music, and fashion become visible and can be analyzed. Recognizing the social production of the imagined world also helps us understand communities of worship as zones of influence among many others.

The church or synagogue exists as a zone offering an imagination of life it claims is not only worth following but salvific, liberating us for a new kind of life. The church, for example, offers life as imagined by Jesus, a Galilean Jew it names as the Christ. Part of the problem of the church in our time is that of offering a compelling religious imagination of life in the face of other agencies offering attractive alternative imaginations. This book is preoccupied with this problem. A particular imagination is viable only when there are people inclined to follow it and willing to face up to the difficulties of doing so.

I have described here briefly the process by which I came to reflect on the problem of the sometimes contradictory influences on young people I worked with as a high school teacher, then later as a parish catechist, and lastly as a university teacher. Of course, these influences affect not just young people but all of us, myself included. As broad social influences, they are properly understood by examining their pervasiveness and the specific human processes that support that pervasiveness. At one point, I decided I needed to find a more systematic, theoretical approach to the various influences shaping consciousness and behavior in our time. In hopes of finding a wide-angle approach to my questions, I started examining various theories of culture. During a year-long sabbatical in 1984–85, I focused on the thought of the Welsh scholar Raymond Williams, who wrote prolifically about culture over a lifetime of creative scholarship. His influence on my own thinking will be obvious throughout this book as I seek to explain and build on his way of approaching culture.

Studying Williams's writings clarified for me two matters. First, culture itself is a complex concept all too easily dealt with in reductionist terms. The correct direction for appraising cultural realities lies in charting their true complexity rather than reducing them to an artificial and ultimately distorting simplicity. This realization helped me see that I did not want to write a book about the concept of culture in general but about a specific aspect of culture: *the way electronic communications, especially film and television, shape our world of meaning.* The conviction underlying this book is that the imagination of human existence communicated via electronic media needs scrutiny and judgment. The procedures by which that imagination is created and fed into our meaning system need to be examined in the light of critical thinking, under which I include religious thinking.

Second, Williams showed me that the best way of helping people see culture as an active rather than a static reality is by focusing on cultural production in any of its various forms. Williams's rule-of-thumb definition of culture stresses it as a system of production of meaning rather than as some vague network of a society's total values and meanings: "Culture is a signifying system by which a social order is communicated, reproduced, experienced, and explored."[3] The system of signification becomes visible in a society's procedures of communication and in the interests they represent or ignore. As we shall see, focusing on the actual processes

by which versions of reality are produced offers the best
angle from which to see and judge these versions. The production of signification, rather than its "consumption" or
reception, will be the main focus of this book. Unless the system by which meaning is produced can be noticed, it cannot
be thought about and analyzed.

In a theater I watch a film that begins with a woman walking alone, soon stalked by a man who brutally murders her.
Later, I realize that a relatively large number of other films
have this same scenario as the main or sub-plot. I mention
the matter to a male friend who tells me that it is not a bad
message, since in fact, a woman alone is a potential victim.
I decide to find out who wrote the screenplays for a sam-
pling of such films and who were the persons involved in
their production. In each case the screenplays were written
by men and cinematically produced by crews in which men
predominated by a ratio of 10 to 1. I begin to think: Men are
imagining for all, women and men alike, what it means to be
a woman today, and it means that a woman alone is a potential victim. A male tells me the scenario is true to life. But
I find myself asking: Does this imagination of women as victims reproduce itself? Does it at some subtle level leave men
imagining that *a woman alone is indeed a potential victim,*
and if so, what are the outcomes of this imagination? Does
it lead some men to imagine women alone as *their* victims?

In this example, I looked first at the production of these
images of women as victims and only then at the way the
images are received by those at the point of consumption.
The point of consumption is much more difficult to analyze,
for the simple reason that symbols, images, and narratives,
written or filmed, tend away from univocal meaning and
toward multiple meanings and multiple effects. If it is possible that the victim films cited here could help men imagine
women as victims, they could also possibly warn women to
be more careful and strengthen their resolve to fight victimization through specific, planned strategies. Even here, one
strategy of women might be to protest these very depictions
of their victimization.

Signification of all kinds, including religious meaning, tends to be multivalent and works in sometimes contradictory ways. This fact cautions us that analysis of the actual reception of various media must be nuanced so as to take account of ambiguous, even contradictory, effects. I will give more attention to this theme at later points in this book, especially in chapters 5 and 6.

The kind of noticing, examination, and analysis in my example is an aspect of cultural agency. Understanding how cultural production works and uncovering the human hands at work in it may also show particular persons and groups that they can move beyond being passive consumers of others' significations. They can undertake the production of meaning themselves, first by becoming questioners of the products handed them for their consumption and then by becoming co-creators of their own versions of the world.

To be helpful, then, an attempt to deal with culture and electronic communications will need careful distinctions essential for understanding how the production of culture works and its relation to cultural consumption. In the end these distinctions will be the gauges for whatever value this book may have, since my overall goal here is to foster the kind of cultural agency made possible by a grasp of culture as a signifying system.

The opposite of cultural agency is cultural oppression, the imposition of a world of meaning on others in such a way that they cannot think about it or question it. In our day such oppression takes the form of "a tyranny of images," defining for the unwitting the shape of their lives. This book seeks to disrupt the tyranny of images operating in collusion with political and economic tyrannies.[4] Raymond Williams's overall approach to culture stresses cultural agency, and in this, his work is similar to that of Paulo Freire, whose writings Williams seems not to have known. In this introductory chapter, I set the stage for the examination of cultural agency throughout this book by a brief overview of Freire's work on this matter.

## Cultural Action/Cultural Agency

Many readers may know of the work of the Brazilian educator Paulo Freire, who initiated a revolution in the way many persons, particularly educators, think about culture. Freire was a professor of educational history and theory at the University of Recife in Northeast Brazil until 1964. Since the late 1940s he had been paying attention to the problems of adult literacy in his country.[5] Early on he became dissatisfied with the most commonly used methods for teaching reading to adults. The reading primers for beginners ignored the social realities lived by the adults learning to read. They were more similar to the material used by children, about dogs and cats and running and jumping. Freire saw that these materials suppressed among these adults a chance to understand the condition of their own poverty and oppression. If literacy is a process of naming, then why not help adults engage in a more original naming of the conditions of their own lives and the causes of those conditions?

Eventually Freire developed a process for teaching literacy that gave socially marginal people a way of naming their own oppressed situation and, in the process, a way of questioning how it had come about and how it could be reversed. He began theorizing about what he was doing as a form of "cultural action for freedom," a phrase that later became the title of one of his essay collections.[6] This sort of cultural action made some in Brazil nervous, and in 1964 a U.S.-supported military coup curtailed the more than twenty thousand literacy circles teaching adults to read and write by helping them find the words to name their oppression.[7] Moving to Chile, Freire was able to continue his internationally acclaimed work.[8]

When Freire's writings first started appearing in English, many people familiar enough with the idea of political action had not considered the possibility of cultural action. *Cultural Action for Freedom*, like all his writings, examines the process by which people submerged in a particular system of meanings, values, customs, traditions, and so forth, can eventually come to see that this system has been humanly produced. A signifying system is a culture, a human construct that names the world the way some particular person, group, or groups, usually those with money and power, want it named. Freire realized that most people assume a posture of powerlessness and passivity before a system of meanings. They are not aware of the possibility of cultural action, that is, of the active work of questioning, contesting, and even restructuring the system of meanings.

In Freire's work with the illiterate poor, their concrete situation of misery was the fulcrum providing them the leverage to pry the weight of oppressive understandings — and eventually the oppressive system itself — off their backs. If misery was the fulcrum, examining and renaming reality was the lever. With the weight of oppressive versions of reality removed, people could stand upright and begin to direct their own lives. What provided the impulse for using the lever in the first place was the realization that the social world is humanly constructed, that it is *someone's system,* not divinely ordained or "natural" like the contours of the land.

Freire uses the term "praxis" for an approach to reality that bonds proper theory with action for liberation. In praxis, action is the fiery cauldron that melts down theory and tests its mettle for both its potential value and its possible correction. What is often overlooked in accounts of Freire's work is his belief that *the very examination* of meanings and values and ways of proceeding *is* praxis; it is a significant kind of action in itself. Freire, in his approach to engaging and questioning meaning, puts a high value on the seminal action of paying attention. To speak in a nuanced way of this kind of action calls for an expanded language only now being created.

A term I will use often in this book to suggest a way of thinking and acting about electronically communicated messages is "cultural agency."[9] Not so different from Freire's "cultural action," the term connotes the continuing possibility of making judgments and then decisions about what we will or will not listen to or see. True judgment is always critical in the sense of discerning quality or the lack of it, but it is not always negative. Far from it. Mark Miller, writing specifically about television, reminds us of the double, positive-negative poles to critique. Using the word "read" to mean critical discernment, Miller says:

> To read is not just to undo. Critical analysis can just as easily reclaim a marvel, reveal — in all humility — some excellence obscured by time and preconception, as it can devastate a lie. And . . . the critical impulse can help also to replenish the minds within its sphere. Contrary to an old McLuhanite canard, those who have grown up watching television are not, because of all that gaping, now automatically adept at visual interpretation. That spectatorial "experience" is passive, mesmeric, undiscriminating, and therefore not conducive to the refinement of the critical faculties: logic and imagination, linguistic precision, historical awareness, and a capacity for long, intense absorption. These — and not the abilities to compute, apply or memorize — are the true desiderata of any higher education, and it is critical thinking that can best realize them.[10]

As used here, cultural agency does not mean that a person simply makes a decision to pick up a newspaper or turn on the TV or the radio. A person can do such things without possessing cultural agency, that is, without being a cultural subject directing one's life with intention. Cultural agency is a matter of knowing — or working to know — which aspects of the meaning system one will accept and which ones one will resist. This book itself is my own effort at cultural agency and an attempt to call others to the task.

Cultural agency happens when a person decides to exercise some judgment and control over the kinds of cultural material s/he will accept and the kinds that must be resisted. In a time when every sort of meaning and value can find its way into one's home electronically, via radio, TV, audio and video cassette, and compact disc, cultural agency is not so common as one would hope. In fact many studies confirm that cultural passivity is the norm for most persons, what Miller above referred to as "passive, mesmeric, undiscriminating." Thus, once the television is switched on in the evening in most homes, it tends to stay tuned to the same channel for the rest of the evening. Knowing this, network planners put special emphasis on scheduling an attractive program early in the evening. Robert Kubey's studies of TV viewing patterns verify the role of passivity there. Acknowledging relaxation as the main benefit of viewing, he found relaxed passivity so pronounced that viewers commonly cannot turn off the set. Ironically, the more people watch, the more dissatisfied they are with what they are watching and the more disinterested in it. "Viewing begets more viewing because one must keep watching in order to remain relaxed. A kind of psychological and physical inertia develops."[11]

However, limited forms of cultural agency are not uncommon, and even in their partialness are still valuable. Thus some people decide they will not purchase or look at pornography, or that they will not watch certain violent films or will not allow TV vulgarity into their homes. Many examples of limited cultural agency can be found among parents trying to offer children a humanizing imagination of the world. Some parents exercise such agency with regard to the cultural products their children have access to. They monitor the music, films, and other visual narratives their children watch or listen to, and make choices about the kinds of toys they permit to their children. While many parents select toys primarily on the issue of cost and packaging, some examine the import of the toy itself, not allowing military toys or those that hinder group play or that require minimal creative activity on the part of the child.

There was a time — and I do not care to grieve nostalgically for it — when versions of the world did not come into one's home unless one went out and brought them in. A book, which would always present a version of reality (and also one "concocted" by a person the reader might never meet), had to be purchased and then brought across the threshold of the home by some person. The same would be true of a song, which also offers a version of reality: it could only enter the home through some person. Today, however, once the TV or radio has been brought into the home and plugged in, its versions of reality enter the home, not across the threshold but in a quite different electronic way, offering a new kind of accessibility to multiple versions of reality.

The new electronic communications technology re-shapes the environments of our homes. When this technology is used without responsible insight, that shaping of our environment can be harmful to us or at least can have unforeseen consequences. Parents whose home is hooked up to a cable network decide their nine-year-old daughter may have a TV in her bedroom at the top of the house. They have decided to allow her, once in that room alone, unsupervised access at any hour to a range of televisual "entertainment," some of it unsuitable to one her age. The decision to allow the TV in the bedroom has behavioral implications not so much because there may be unseemly programming on it but because the decision shifts the relational patterns between child and parents, among others in the home, and ultimately, the pattern of influences. The child of nine may now find herself in the electronic hands of persons who imagine for her the shape of the human, persons her parents might never have allowed into their home had they met them first.[12]

Full cultural agency, especially as I wish to propose it in this book, has two aspects. It is an active way of looking at and making decisions about the meanings and values created for us in our society, but it is also an active way of examining and judging the *channels* by which these meanings and values are communicated to us. Seen this way, cultural agency embraces as a basic tool cultural analysis: the ability to bring cultural products and their latent imagination of life before the "tribunal of judgment" to assess their value or appropriateness. As a parent, a person moves toward full cultural agency by examining all the ways the world is imagined for a child, but also works to help the child herself think actively about them. Ironically, some bring to the selection of their electronics equipment stringent technical criteria and a sophisticated analysis of technical specifications but apply almost no criteria or analysis to the material that comes to them via this equipment.

A parent who is a cultural agent might view visual material with the child in order to maintain some kind of active dialogue about the images and narratives provided there. But the parent would also be concerned about the kinds of adult persons who visit the home and interact with children. Persons can be intentionally gathered around the dinner table with that interaction in mind. Family customs may embrace the preparation and use of food, events for and styles of celebration, ways of remembering family history, patterns for taking vacations, even the sorts of games played, all seeking to provide a rich world of meaning in which the child is not a passive spectator. Implied in this description of the parent is a person who embodies cultural agency as a habitual way of understanding and interacting with the world in which we live. As cultural agents, parents consciously shape the tastes of children, a task involving years of painstaking attention. To use a culinary metaphor for "taste," at the opposite pole of such agency might be an unspoken policy of "leaving it to McDonald's" to shape children's tastes.

I agree with Freire's belief that each person's vocation is to be a subject, not an object. A subject is a person able to engage in the humanizing process of liberation which includes dialogue and action for change; a person as object is one reduced to be a passive receptor of the wishes and desires of others: a slave. This question of cultural agency is one I will return to again in the following pages. My effort in this book is to provide a way of seeing and dealing with the cultural oppression that may come from electronic communications. However, it should be clear that at no point am I suggesting that all electronic communications or what I call "the wider culture" are oppressive.

## Problems for Religious Traditions

It is only fairly late in the twentieth century, decades after the basic electronic communications technologies were in place and widely used as channels for ever more persuasive narratives, that various religious groups have sounded an alarm over the power of these media to subvert their own agenda.[13] Thinkers in religious traditions are probing the effects of media on the consciousness of their people, a sign that the full power of electronic communications' influence is finally dawning on those who propose particular religious commitments. The *religious* significance of George Gerbner's claim that television and not parents now tell children (and everyone else) most of the stories most of the time is becoming clearer to religious groups, all of which have a story that seeks to direct in a compelling way their adherents' outlook on life. That story can and in many cases does conflict with the vivid stories told in various media.

Religious groups are not alone in these concerns, such as when the non-religiously affiliated National Coalition on Television Violence points out that the 500–600 percent rise in U.S. violence since the 1950s actually began in 1956–57, the year when TV violence escalated.[14] Violence is a concern of many in society, religiously affiliated or not. Still, when that concern is honed by religious values, as one might expect it to be, say, in the churches committed to follow Jesus' proposals of compassion and non-violence, the concern can have a sharper edge to it. Religious leaders are finding that the electronically imagined world can be in direct conflict with the religiously imagined world and thus needs special attention. Pope John Paul II, for example, has defined oppression in the First World as mainly cultural, that is, involving its system of values and signification.[15] Concern for faith in time of potential cultural oppression is a dominant feature of the writings of this religious leader.

## Religion as a Culture

If, as Raymond Williams claims, a culture is a signifying system, then we have to recognize that a religion too is a signifying system. As a zone of signification, a religion is in fact a culture, though the way it is a culture needs careful explanation. As a culture with a specific vision of the world, the church, synagogue, or mosque still exists within the wider culture and takes many of its human values from that wider culture. It does not invent, for instance, the words it uses in its own speech about God. Those words are spoken in the language that has emerged socially and culturally over centuries in a process that goes far beyond its own assembly of worship. A particular religious group, then, while affirming its own specific vision of reality, must also affirm all the authentically good values found in the wider culture and be in active dialogue with those values. If all good is not found exclusively in the synagogue or church, neither is all evil found exclusively in society. A religion as a human institution can only struggle to live up to its own vision, to reform continually its life so as to be coherent with its vision.[16] At the same time, it admits to its many failures, some of which have been a scandal to non-members and remain as historical evidence of its own institutional evil.

Still the fact remains that a particular religion itself represents a distinctive zone of signification, a culture, that exists within a wider culture. We have in fact *two* cultures, each wanting allegiance. These claims to allegiance inevitably create tensions. A religion is more specific and intentional in its meanings than the wider culture, but on the other hand, its claims about its meanings are broader and more explicit.[17] For its meanings and significations a religion claims ultimacy and an ultimate kind of allegiance. Explicitly and overtly, a religion says: "These meanings and values are the decisive ones for life; they are salvific." Such a claim to ultimate meaning is also a claim to be able to judge reality by those ultimate norms. Speaking specifically about Christianity, a theologian put the matter the following way:

...It is a perception as old as Christianity that faith in Jesus Christ brings freedom. As the inner freedom of the Spirit, it is a life-force for a person and for a people that gives rise to new perceptions, new relations, new ways of being, free from fear, free from restrictive attachments, free from oppressive external pressures. As a social force, this freedom always enabled Christian communities to take up new positions on such issues as slavery, marriage customs, military service, the place of women and children in society, and the like. Looked at from today's point of view, we sometimes seem to feel that the Gospel was not lived radically enough in the past, that other cultural forces seem to have prevailed over the freedom of the Gospel. However, whatever historical judgments we make it is important to note that the Gospel was often a force pushing from within a culture to adopt new ways, or even to revise a whole philosophy of life and cosmos.[18]

What must be added to the issue of religion as a culture with claims to ultimacy is that the wider culture also claims ultimacy for its meanings, though it does so in an implicit way. Ironically, implicit claims tend to be more persuasive than explicit ones. The covert claim, never openly made but quietly assumed, can have greater power because, never explicit, it is harder to resist. When the wider culture's covert ultimacy is set forth in the vivid terms made possible by electronic communications, religion can experience crisis. More and more of those who say they are religious can take life's ultimate meaning not from religious understandings, but from the wider culture.

When contrasting claims are made by each culture, i.e., the religious one and the wider one within which it stands, with each demanding allegiance to its understandings, something has to give. There are contrasting responses to the dilemma. Some religious persons take a stance of commitment to their religious principles, resisting and rejecting the unacceptable values. In extreme instances, this resistance leads to the martyr's death. More commonly, others quietly, and perhaps not even fully consciously, push their religious commitments aside when these conflict with the wider culture. Another form of capitulation, more subtle and likely more common, is to reduce one's religious understandings to the point where they no longer conflict with those of the wider culture. Such a strategy can be used by whole groups or communities and not just by individual persons.

For Christians, this last step must always affect the way Jesus is understood. As found in scripture, Jesus' life proposes taking the side of the victims and questioning the social structures that collude in their victimization. His teaching disrupts the covert ultimacy of social arrangements and turns the popular wisdom on its head. His way is one that ignores social barriers, casts suspicion on the accumulation of wealth, and proposes non-retaliation for offenses. Jesus' imagination of the possibilities of life, never easily maintained in any period of history, can be especially difficult to face in a time when social status, wealth, and domination are all prized and continually reinforced in electronic narratives. Rather than face this Jesus, we can easily invent a "Jesus reduction program," producing a diminished Jesus who neatly fits the aspirations of middle-class persons. Like his followers working for justice in Central and South America, the Jesus of justice and peace is "disappeared" in the very churches where his Spirit is to live. When Jesus' disciples allow this to happen, they award the true decisive ultimacy to the wider culture. The history of the church shows this struggle between the two cultures to be a persistent one.

## The Religious Culture as a Culture of Resistance

In a time when the wider culture's meanings and values, both positive and negative, are communicated through the incessant and vivid imagery of electronic media, it seems more and more likely that religious groups will retain their vision and way of life only by becoming centers of cultural resistance to those elements in the wider culture not acceptable to their religious insight. Such resistance does not call us to take the world less seriously but more so. It seeks to escape not the world but the trivialization of the world by which other persons become instruments of my self-will rather than temples of the living God. Love of the world in its best possibilities has deep roots in most religions.

Resistance is a necessary form of any true cultural agency. In his book *We Drink from Our Own Wells,* Peruvian theologian Gustavo Gutiérrez examines the sort of spirituality of resistance needed by the poor and politically marginal people of Latin America. Early on, Gutiérrez uses a telling phrase to name the effort of the powerful to withdraw from the poor every source of meaning and value that gives them strength. He calls this effort a work of "cultural death." Opposing and countering such a cultural death is the deep, life-giving spirituality accessible to the poor through religious symbols. This is a spirituality that reveres the dignity of each person and calls each to ratify that dignity in the struggle for justice. Gutiérrez's title, *We Drink from Our Own Wells,* offers a compelling metaphor for the spirit-sustaining possibilities of religious groups as zones of signification. Implied in his title is the importance of refusing to imbibe cultural pollution, with its false and poisoning versions of human life, concocted by unseen elites. This asceticism of disengagement is to be bonded to an asceticism of engagement. In the latter, people have access to their own wells, their own versions of reality, and their own sources of cultural life and nourishment.[19]

A religion, then, embodies a vision, and its rituals and disciplines are designed to enable people to focus their attention on this vision. Since attention is not automatic, all religions have procedures to maintain attention on matters not immediately obvious to all. A commentator on the internationalization of communications suggests why attention-maintenance might be so important to religious persons today:

One of the most profitable commodities in the modern world is human attention. Whoever can harvest it in wholesale quantities can make money in kind. In the United States, one Nielsen rating point reflects 1 percent of the country's 90 million television households. One percentage point for a network in prime-time audience share represents more than $30 million in added revenues each year. Nothing in human experience has prepared men, women, and children for the modern television techniques of fixing human attention and creating the uncritical mood required to sell goods, many of which are marginal at best to human needs.[20]

Bagdikian's warning shows why some hold that the crisis of the human spirit in our time is, in part, a crisis of knowing what matters are worthy of our attention. In a privately circulated memo, religious writer Gary MacEoin gives us some idea of who controls this orchestration of attention:

Ten business and financial corporations control the three major radio and TV networks, 34 subsidiary TV stations, 200 cable TV systems, 62 radio stations, 20 record companies, 59 magazines (including *Time* and *Newsweek*), 58 newspapers (including the *New York Times, Washington Post, Wall Street Journal, Los Angeles Times*), 41 book publishers, and several film producers and distributors.... Ten corporations now earn more than half of all newspaper revenue in the U.S.[21]

MacEoin claims these media work hard to maintain "at all costs" their image as the watchdog of the public interest, whereas in fact they highlight the role of the President and his immediate staff as symbols of power. Tied to the obvious issue here of political discourse are other issues affecting the human spirit. Religious people will do well to be aware of the commodification of their attention and of the need to resist it.

More implicit in Gutiérrez's book title than his metaphor of pollution is a distinction between *the culture of the people and the culture concocted for the consumption of the people.* When a people find ways of expressing their own sense of themselves in song, story, jokes, anecdotes, proverbs, dance, and so forth, they are co-producing their own culture. Should a people ever become dependent on the imaginations of reality produced for their consumption by unseen persons feeding them a diet of images, narratives, songs, etc. that basically silence them, they lose a key feature of their own humanization. They cease in some sense to be subjects naming and celebrating their own distinctive life and instead become objects, with their life's meaning handed them by others. When some use the term "popular culture," what they mean is not the culture in Gutiérrez's sense, bubbling out of a people, but the culture fed to them by others.[22] This problem of cultural consumption is a large one, and I will return to this matter later in this book.

In *We Drink from Our Own Wells*, Gutiérrez examines the dramatic choices that must be made in situations of oppression: opting for the false promises of oppressors and their dehumanizing consequences, or for the liberating, life-sustaining message of the Gospel. Sometimes, however, the choices are not so black and white, with the religious culture true and good and the wider culture false. The secular, non-religious culture always possesses life-enriching characteristics valuable to religious persons, a matter I will deal with at greater length in the following chapter. As one example among many, Educators for Social Responsibility, an organization with no formal religious affiliation, has done more to help young people understand global issues and the possibilities of peace than have some religious denominations. On the other hand, religious groups themselves need to monitor and purify their wells to protect themselves from pollutants like patriarchy, homophobia, militarism, and consumerism, or even fanaticism. My own hunch about the process of maintaining a nourishing religious culture is that it involves the participation of all in an ongoing search for deeper understanding and for deeper commitments.

In clarifying further the religious zone of signification as a culture of resistance, I wish to treat somewhat briefly two matters of importance to the pursuit of a distinctive religious vision: life structure and the imagery that supports it. Here I am proposing two theorems, first, that life structure supports culture, whether a religious or a consumerist one; second, that images support life structure. Both matters are important for grasping the task of cultural agency in religious groups today. Later chapters of this book work to further nuance our understanding of the relationship among religious cultural agency, life structure, and images.

## Religious Vision and Life Structure

Lived commitments are the key to religious resistance. An underlying conviction throughout Gutiérrez's book is that a spirituality of resistance is much more a way of living than a way of thinking. A religious culture of resistance is impossible unless grounded in patterned ways of living that embody an alternative vision of life. Patterned ways of living are what I call "life structure." The problem of cultural resistance in many religious groups today is one of finding, at both communal and individual personal levels, life structures coherent with stated commitments.

The functioning of life structure becomes clearer when looked at in the life of a particular person. A life structure is a pattern of choices and ways of living that becomes the established mode for a person. Once established, the pattern tends to perdure, even in spite of shifts in location, career, or marriage partner. A helpful explanation of life structure is offered by Daniel Levinson:

> By life structure we mean the underlying pattern or design of a person's life at a given time.... A life has many components: occupation, love relationships, marriage and family, relation to oneself, use of solitude, roles in various social contexts — all the relationships with individuals, groups and institutions that have sig-

nificance for a person. One's personality influences and is influenced by involvement with each of them.... The concept of life structure — the basic pattern or design of a person's life at a given time — gives us a way of looking at the engagement of the individual in society. It requires us to consider both self and world, and the relationships between them.[23]

Levinson draws our attention to the patterns that tend to direct one's life.

These would include patterns in the use of time; tastes in food; preferences and even styles of watching TV; ways of being with people, older, younger, peers; ways of behaving in groups; ways of studying, of reading, even of reading the newspaper — or the patterns of not doing any of these things. One could take almost any aspect of life and examine the life patterns there that eventually combine to form a life structure: ways of driving a car, ways of using alcohol, ways of relating to the opposite sex, ways of dealing with the truth, ways of getting one's own way, and especially, ways of thinking about and using money. Behind the nexus of these patterns is a life structure that affects commitments.

Are such patterns formed unconsciously? Are they outside of what I have called agency? I doubt it. They are all based at some point on choices, though to be sure many of these choices are made aimlessly or at least without full advertence to their potential consequences.[24] These choices are also heavily influenced by the imaginations offered us about what the shape of our lives should be. John Kavanaugh has shown how closely the electronic imagery of advertising is related to unfettered industrial capitalism and how it affects the lifestyle of consumption.[25] In this case, the production of meaning is closely tied to the production of consumption.

For religious groups, cultural agency would involve working with questions of life structure, both at the level of the community's institutional life patterns and of the individual members. The task of redirecting life structure is no small one, considering the pressures of the marketeers alluded to above. Even to get to the task, the Christian churches have to reverse their reluctance to deal with life patterns, except perhaps in matters affecting sexual practices. Having listened to sermons for many years, I have found the question of life structure to be rarely broached, let alone dealt with. When this task is faced, there will be no formulas to guide the way. Even so, the most usual path may be one of first coming to see the Gospel's vision as radically alternative to the vision of the wider culture, and then shifting the pattern of one's life so as to be in keeping with one's vision.[26] The reformulation of either, the vision or the pattern of action, involves a new level of agency. A religious tradition that forfeits such agency enters deep crisis, since

> a religion fades out of history when its symbols and institutions lose their capacity to evoke among its followers the distinctive salvific experience [including its behavioral consequences] that defines its essence. Did not this happen to the great religions of ancient Egypt, Rome, Greece, and Mesopotamia?[27]

Once recognized, the importance of life structure for religious living calls us to pay attention to the material conditions of individuals and groups. These conditions are specific and can be studied for their coherence or lack of it with the stated vision of the group. Thus if, for example, Christians accept the importance of Matthew 25 as a normative text for Christian living, then their material conditions must be carefully examined to determine whether or not they facilitate or hinder fidelity to those ideals.

In summary, then, one gets access to the actual culture of religious groups by examining their life structure, rather than their explicit verbal claims. In the religious realm, a group does not think itself into ways of acting but acts itself into ways of thinking. Many of the procedures used in religious groups simply reproduce the structures of the wider society.[28] In a society enjoying its economic privilege thanks to the domination enforced by massive armaments, religious leadership might find dominative, patriarchal power

"normal" for its religious adherents. In a society where selection of the right products subtly becomes the yardstick of
wisdom, religious doctrines themselves can become a kind
of product retailed by the "company." In this case, the
faithful are not allowed to become co-producers of the religious culture, but only passive consumers.[29] Obviously such
an arrangement subverts the search for religious wisdom
through inquiry. Again and again, social researchers have
found socio-economic status a more profound influence on
religious groups than their stated doctrines.[30]

However, not all religious groups adopt a life structure
that apes the patterns of the wider society. Some drink deeply
from the well of their sacred writings, ingesting from them
a way of living distinctively in keeping with the norms of
those texts. World wide among Christians, the option for the
poor is pushing some groups to shift their life structure. Life
structure is founded on commitments. When a group tries to
commit itself to the marginalized or the victims and begins
to view the world through their eyes, its way of life changes.
Find the right commitments and the right life structure will
follow.

## Images and Life Structure

The second matter I wish to clarify somewhat briefly here is
how images support life structure. Later, in chapter 5, I will
deal extensively with images and how they can be classified
and analyzed. In this chapter, I have used phrases like "Jesus'
imagination of life's possibilities" and "the imagery of advertising," and I have applauded Gutiérrez's metaphor of
the well. Behind such language is the following assumption
about culture: Underlying any culture is a way of imagining
the world. The cultural system and the life structure supporting it are themselves supported by a system of images. Get at
that image system, and one has gotten at part of the inner
core of culture. We could accurately say, "You'll know what
is in their hearts by the images and metaphors they use to

speak of it." Persons are always revealing their assumptions about reality through what they say after "like" or "as." The sort of images I am speaking of here are not so much the images we see as those *by which* we see, that is, images serving as cultural lenses through which we perceive reality. It is very difficult to shift life structure unless there is a parallel shift in the way one imagines the world.

Should we find that the images controlling the imaginations of persons who like to name themselves religious are the irreligious images of competition and even violent domination, then we at least know the scope of our problem. Among Christians, a good example of this problem can be found in actual celebrations of the Eucharist, when, over and over again, the assembly affirms its "oneness," using varied synonyms for unity. Yet for many, the meaning of "one" is not a unity with sisters and brothers throughout the world, but "one," as in "We're number one." The unitive "one" of the Eucharist is at fundamental odds with the competitive "one" of domination. Unfortunately, the Eucharistic "one" can be vastly overridden by dominant images of winning, of getting ahead, of success, of having more, and so forth. Jesus is meant to be the bond of unity, not the point of domination. On the contrary, Jesus bonded with the victims. Yet, for many persons living in a culture of competition and domination, the competitive "one" so overrides the unitive "one" that it almost disappears, and with it, the deepest call of the Gospel. Though it may be on the lips, the human unity proclaimed by Jesus does not affect the heart.

The rest of this book will deal with how culture functions and its relationship to religious groups, including groups of Christians seeking to follow Jesus in a time of electronic amplification. Up to this point, for those who wish to begin developing the skills of cultural analysis, I have suggested: (1) Pay attention to the images that support culture; (2) examine the life structures that support culture, particularly the commitments hidden in life structure; (3) pay attention to how any particular aspect of culture is produced, trying to name the process and find the actual persons who have a part in any point in that process. However, beyond all of these, a stance of resistance to all that is inhuman, to all that violates human unity and human dignity, will help one to see clearly what in the wider culture a religious person cannot accept. Like all the great religious leaders, Jesus lived such a stance, and that is why for his disciples, Jesus is the touchstone of cultural analysis.

In the next chapter I wish to deal with the concept of culture in greater detail, first as to the history of the concept and then in its relationship to religious groups and, in chapter 3, to schools. A grasp of the idea of culture is the foundation of the ability to see how culture actually functions.

## Notes

1. Henri Marrou, *A History of Education in Antiquity,* trans. George Lamb (Madison: University of Wisconsin Press, 1982), p. 147.

2. George Gerbner, "The Challenge of Television," unpublished paper, Annenberg School of Communication, University of Pennsylvania, p. 8.

3. Raymond Williams, *The Sociology of Culture* (New York: Schocken Books, 1982), p. 13.

4. The phrase "tyranny of images" is from Michael D. Higgins. See M. D. Higgins, "The Tyranny of Images: Aspects of Hidden Control — Literature, Ethnography, and Political Commentary in the West of Ireland," *The Crane Bag* (Dublin) 8, no. 2 (1984): 132–42.

5. A series of conversations between Freire and Myles Horton provide rich material on Freire's own history. See Brenda Bell, John Gaventa, and John Peters, eds., *We Make the Road by Walking: Myles Horton and Paulo Freire: Conversations on Education and Social Change* (Philadelphia: Temple University Press, 1990).

6. Paulo Freire, *Cultural Action for Freedom* (Cambridge, Mass.: Harvard Educational Review and the Center for the Study of Development and Social Change, Monograph Series no. 1, 1970). The essays in this booklet can also be found under separate titles as chapters 6 and 7 of Paulo Freire, *The Politics of Education* (Granby, Mass.: Bergin and Garvey, 1985).

7. Here I am following the eighteen page monograph by Thomas Sanders, "The Paulo Freire Method," American Universities Field Staff Reports, West Coast South America Series 15, no. 1 (Hanover, N.H., 1968).

8. There are dozens of critical appraisals of Freire's work. A useful recent one is: John L. Elias, *Paulo Freire: Pedagogue of Liberation* (Melbourne, Fla.: Krieger Publishing Co., 1994).

9. See the brief but valuable comment on how people can act as cultural agents in, Gregory Baum, "Option for the Powerless," *The Ecumenist* 26, no. 1 (November–December 1987): 5–11, at p. 9, col. 2.

10. Mark Crispin Miller, *Boxed-In: The Culture of TV* (Evanston, Ill.: Northwestern University Press, 1988), p. 6.

11. Robert Kubey, "A Body at Rest Tends to Remain Glued to the Tube," *New York Times* (5 August 1990): H 47.

12. See the analysis of such decisions in Albert Borgmann, *Crossing the Postmodern Divide* (Chicago: University of Chicago Press, 1993), pp. 110–26.

13. Three examples from U.S. churches are: National Council of the Churches of Christ in the USA, *Violence and Sexual Violence in Film, Television, Cable, and Home Video,* Report of a Study Commission of the Communication Commission (New York: Communication Commission, National Council of Churches, 1985); Mary Lou Schropp, ed., *Platform for Action: The Electronic Media, Popular Culture and Family Values* (New York: United States Catholic Conference, Department of Communication, 1985). Another, more recent, example is the report of the National Council of Churches Study Commission on Theology, Education, and the Electronic Media, featured in a special issue of the journal *Religious Education* 82, no. 2 (1987).

14. National Coalition on Television Violence, "NCTV Estimate on Impact of Violence," *NCTV News* 8, nos. 3–4 (July–August 1987).

15. See the interpretation of the Pope's speeches in Canada in Gregory Baum, "The Labor Pope in Canada," *The Ecumenist* 23, no. 2 (January–February 1985): 17–23.

16. In fact the very nature of the church blends historical reality with what Edward Farley calls "ideality," a reality not yet realized and indeed not yet possible of realization. See Edward Farley, *Ecclesial Reflection: An Anatomy of Theological Method* (Philadelphia: Fortress Press, 1982), pp. 219–20.

17. In distinguishing the two cultures, I have no wish to imply that a particular religious system has somehow existed in some timeless, unsullied state, uninfluenced by wider societies and their cultures. Religion is always so influenced, at the same time it judges the wider society and rejects values at variance with its own. The relationship is complex. For some striking examples of this complexity, see any of the novels or plays of the Roman Catholic Japanese writer Shusaku Endo. Also, in this book, Christianity is my usual example of a religion and my chief concern as well. However, I do not use "religion" as a synonym for Christianity.

18. David Power, "Liturgy and Culture," *East Asian Pastoral Review* 21, no. 4 (1984): 348–60, at 348–49.

19. See the eloquent statement of Jon Sobrino, "Evil and Hope: A Reflection from the Victims," Catholic Theological Society of America, *Proceedings* 50 (1995): 71–84.

20. Ben H. Bagdikian, "The Lords of the Global Village," *The Nation* (12 June 1989): 805–20, at 819.

21. Privately circulated memo, 19 September 1985. The control of these media is in even fewer hands today.

22. This is the use I find in Andrew Greeley, *A Theology of Popular Culture* (Chicago: Thomas More, 1988). I have found no other single book that is such a polar opposite to my own thinking about culture.

23. Daniel Levinson, *The Seasons of a Man's Life* (New York: Alfred A. Knopf, 1978), pp. 41–42. Levinson's study is specifically of men, and I have adjusted his prose here so as to be more inclusive. See also, more recently, Daniel Levinson, with Judy D. Levinson, *The Seasons of a Woman's Life* (New York: Knopf, 1996).

24. Levinson highlights the matter of choices the following way:

> How shall we go about describing and analyzing the life structure? The most useful starting point . . . is to consider the choices a person makes and how s/he deals with their consequences. The important choices in adult life have to do with work, family, friendships, and love relationships of various kinds, where to live, leisure, involvement in religious, political, and community life, immediate and long term goals. (*Man's Life,* p. 43)

25. John Kavanaugh, "The World of Wealth and the Gods of Wealth," in Boff and Elizondo, eds., *Option for the Poor: Challenge to the Rich Countries. Concilium* 187 (1986), pp. 17–23.

26. One of the better statements of the need for this effort is Margaret Miles, "The Recovery of Asceticism," *Commonweal* (28 January 1983): 40–43.

27. Aloysius Pieris, "Christianity and Buddhism in Core-to-Core Dialogue," *Cross Currents* 37, no. 1 (Spring 1987): 57.

28. See my own essay, "The Worshiping Assembly: Possible Zone of Cultural Contestation," *Worship* 63, no. 1 (January 1989): 2–16. Also, *Faith, Culture, and the Worshiping Community* (Washington, D.C.: Pastoral Press, 1993).

29. An interesting example of a religious congregation being expected to function as consumers but not producers of their own understanding occurred in late 1986 in the Diocese of Brooklyn. A group calling itself the Concerned Catholics of Brooklyn planned a public forum on the case of Archbishop Raymond Hunthausen of Seattle. Bishop Mugavero of Brooklyn announced that "we have had enough dialogue already," and would

allow only prayer but not public discussion of the Hunthausen case. So not only did this bishop decide for the people that they would not be able to develop through public dialogue their own positions on this case; he also selected prayer as a form of imposed muteness. See Ari L. Goldman, "Religion Notes," *New York Times,* 30 November 1986, p. 66.

30. I pursue this matter in greater detail but from a different angle in "Life Structure as the Material Conditions of Living: An Ecclesial Task," *New Theology Review* 8, no. 4 (1995): 26–47.

## Chapter 2

# WHAT IS CULTURE?

The concept of culture lies at the center of one of the major areas of concern in modern thought: how consciousness is shaped socially. One might expect that a word of such importance as "culture" would find itself used judiciously in everyday speech. However, many persons use "culture" as a code word to name a large area of reality but with such vagueness as to be unhelpful. In a daily newspaper, we may find the following: "the Cincinnati cultural scene," "our American culture of violence," "homosexual culture," "Hispanic culture," "youth culture," or "the Protestant culture of hard work." Lacking a clear understanding of what culture means, the word can be used in glib ways that hide instead of disclose its deepest issues. In this chapter, I wish to survey the history of the word "culture." This is required in order to give culture the nuance necessary for the sort of cultural agency I wrote of in the last chapter. Then I will set out Raymond Williams's most succinct description of culture and apply it, first, to religious groups as one zone of cultural agency. From that foundation, I will, in the following chapter, apply these ideas to schools, especially religious schools as a second zone of agency. At the outset, however, a word about Raymond Williams himself is appropriate, since I rely so much on his thought.

Raymond Williams (1921–1988) was born in the Black Mountains of Wales, a region with distinctive traditions and proud to have been able to maintain its own language. He was the son of working-class parents: his mother, a homemaker, and his father, a railway signalman. At Cambridge University in the late 1930s, his undergraduate studies in literature were influenced by F. R. Leavis and his conviction that literature could be used to critique industrial society. These studies interrupted by five years as a tank commander in World War II, Williams returned to Cambridge in 1945 to complete his degree. A lifelong student of Marxism, he was vividly aware of how literary "tradition" tended to confirm class advantage and silence the voice of the workers and the poor. Throughout his life he used his literary skills to recover the lost voices of the past, especially those of the laboring class, and to expose versions of reality, written or visual, that propped up economic privilege. Among the themes in his writings the cultural disparagement of the poor has special importance, both for its recurrence and for the passion with which he deals with it. Another of his seminal convictions is that the forms of communication of any society are important features of the material conditions of life in that society. One could understand society through grasping its forms of communication and how they are related to economic and political developments.

After Williams completed his post-war degree at Cambridge, he spent the next fifteen years working in the adult education department at Oxford, an extra-mural division considered academically marginal. It was hardly marginal for Williams, for during those years he set about his ambitious interdisciplinary studies and produced in 1958 *Culture and Society* and then in 1961 *The Long Revolution.* At publication and since, both books found a wide audience. In 1961 he was appointed a lecturer in the English Faculty at Cambridge University, specializing in Elizabethan drama. His many books and essays produced over the next twenty-five years have proved to have an enduring quality and importance in shaping the new discipline of cultural studies.[1]

Till his death in January 1988, Williams's intellectual interests remained wide and his writing prolific. His ability to cross the lines between fields of study is one of the most impressive aspects of his scholarship. When first reading Williams's writings during a sabbatical in 1984–85, I was also auditing a graduate seminar in economics at another university. I was startled to find that all my fellow students, most of them specialists in economics, were familiar with Williams's writings and were busy applying them to economic analysis. Williams was cited in virtually every class. Now, some years later, I find myself in this book seeking to apply Williams's ideas, not to economics or literary history, but to religious groups and to the question of their own cultural agency.

## Understanding Culture

There are ways of thinking about culture that leave it an abstraction so general and vague that one can think the thought "culture" and still be unable to think *about* it. Lacking specificity, the term becomes conceptually inert. Among the various conceptual tools used for understanding the world, this particular type lies covered with dust, untouched because it is not helpful. For Williams, the problem is partly that culture is seen as something in the past or, if in the present, then as something finished and set:

> In most description and analysis, culture and society are expressed in an habitual past tense. The strongest barrier to the recognition of human cultural activity is this immediate and regular conversion of experience into finished products.[2]

Viewing culture as a finished product may perhaps seem helpful in dealing with the history of ideas, but it is a liability when applied to contemporary life.

When we unwittingly convert current social relationships, institutions, and forms of communication into "set" wholes, we have hidden from ourselves the facts of their production, their ongoing activity, and their living influence on us. There are ways of talking about cultural and social developments that leave aside human agency and responsibility for the turns of history. These ways produce a kind of lazy history, filled with generalizations but empty of human faces.

An example of such a set, finished product might be "teen culture." A graduate student announces in a seminar that the young "should be allowed to enjoy their own culture" without having older persons grousing about these "tastes." In so speaking, he has recognized neither how much "teen culture" is produced for the young by persons long out of their teens nor how carefully orchestrated is the selling of this "culture" to the young. Naming teen culture as some set reality that must be taken "as is" hides from us the specific procedures by which it is produced and communicated. The issue of "teen culture" is more complex than any naive "their culture / our culture" dichotomies can disclose. At the very least, a proper understanding of it must distinguish what in it is actually of and from the young and what is concocted for their consumption.

Social relationships, institutions, and forms of communication, all of which are important aspects of culture, tend, when viewed as already finished products and processes, to remove themselves from analysis. Further, they remove themselves from analysis of their connection to us. In reality, these are not just formed processes; they are also *forming processes,* shaping the lives not only of the unnamed masses but of us ourselves. Unable to look at them as the living presences they are, we prefer to disguise them as static concepts and then ignore them. Worse, the human hands that produced the products and the minds that devised the processes in the first place become, not just hidden, but fully unconsidered. This tendency to speak of culture in static terms unconnected to the processes by which culture is produced is not uncommon among academics.[3] I call such usage "inert," because it does not help us notice and name how the living reality of culture works.

By in practice denying the active, formative influence of these social relationships and institutions, we mistakenly separate the social from the personal. The social becomes what is fixed and explicit: institutions, systems, groupings, and so forth. What is present and moving, what seems beyond the fixed and explicit, what is alive, here-and-now, active, subjective — is grasped and categorized as "the personal." A young person takes up, say, a particular style of dress and sees it as a statement of personal choice, of taste. However, this choice may not be fully understandable unless we see its connection to the social institution of advertising, which works for the production of "taste," and ultimately for the production of consumption. The personal cannot be fully grasped except in its connections to the social.[4] To be adequate, a concept of culture must provide a way of looking at the ongoing processes by which meaning is produced and communicated so that the connection between the personal and the social is maintained.

## Culture in Historical Perspective

How can any of us arrive at a more active and useful understanding of culture? Since a large part of the problem stems from the term's vague meaning, the best route lies in examining the history of its usage. An understanding of the shifts in the meaning of the word "culture" provides a kind of conceptual map to guide one's present and future use of it. Though this historical journey is essential, it is not so easy, especially since culture is "one of the two or three most complicated words in the English language."[5] Those who wish to lay a solid foundation for their own study of culture should not skip over the following paragraphs.

An examination of the history of "culture" is not possible without a simultaneous grasp of the history of such allied notions as "society" and "economy." The social realities behind these three words have influenced each other into modern times,[6] with the evolution of any one area working to shape the evolution of the others — right down to the present. In fact, a notion of culture that does not maintain its connections to society and economics will tend to be inadequate. To summarize the problem of understanding culture: it needs to be based on the historical evolution of the concept, which is tied to the evolution of the social structures of culture, which in turn is tied to the evolution of "society" and "economy." The effort to understand these related developments is rewarded with a nuanced grasp of culture as well as a sound basis for doing cultural analysis.

Each of these areas — society, economy, culture — is a comparatively recent development, at least as currently understood. Originally each named a specific *and local* form of human activity. "Society," for example, before it came to name a general system or order, meant an active fellowship, a company (i.e., those who gather together around bread), and "common doing." The term's emphasis was on immediate relationships. "Society" was a conscious alternative to the formal rigidities of an inherited and imposed social order, almost the opposite of our current usage. One can find this understanding of society as fellowship in Ignatius Loyola's naming of his order of Jesuit priests in the sixteenth century. At first he actually called his group, "The *Company* of Jesus," to suggest a close-knit fellowship, before selecting the synonymous title, "Society of Jesus," as its final name. The word "economy" had a similar specific and local meaning. Long before it came to mean a system of production, distribution, and exchange, it meant the management of a household and later of a community. In this usage, "economy" was a conscious attempt to understand and control activities that were necessary aspects of local, even domestic, reality. This "domestic" usage survives to this day in monasteries, where the person in charge of the kitchen and other household matters is called the "econome."

Originally "culture" also had a localized meaning. It meant the growth and tending of crops and animals, i.e., cultivation, and later, by extension, the growth and tending of human faculties. This root meaning of culture is particularly valuable to keep in mind, since it reminds us that culture is a human work, sown and tilled by human hands. If we trained ourselves on hearing the word "culture" to ask immediately "What human hands are at work here, how, and why?" we would be well on our way to the sort of mental habit needed for cultural analysis. Originally, these meanings were all concrete and particular — limited. To understand them today means allowing ourselves to face their abstract and complex current character as it evolved over time, while also noting the specific ways they actually function in particular instances.

Many people still want to understand culture as a noun of process, i.e., the culture *of* something, no longer of crops or animals but of minds. They wish to think of culture as the cultivation of taste in music, graphic arts, literature, and so forth. This meaning for culture actually developed in the eighteenth century, when it was a term interchangeable with "civilization." The Enlightenment saw civilization as an achievement of historical progress in heightened refinement and order, with obvious implications for defining the superior classes and distinguishing them from the inferior classes. Enlightenment thinkers found the prime examples of such achievement in the metropolitan civilizations of France and England. There "civilized," cultured life was the way of heightened rationality, whose opposite was barbarism. In this elitist sense, some "have" culture and others, the "common people," do not. This snobbish use continues to the present day as probably the most common one for culture. A magazine ad for "cultural vacations in Ireland" explains that one will stay in refurbished castles and dine elegantly to the accompaniment of violin music. Thus, culture means "refined" and expensive. Vintners commonly use culture this way in hawking the "taste" needed to appreciate their wares.

However, even before the end of the eighteenth century, the Enlightenment idea of rational order became vulnerable to questions put to it by new thinkers. Rousseau, and later, Romanticism, attacked "civilization" as artificial when compared with the superiority of nature and "the natural." In this view, natural human needs and impulses were judged more integral to life and thus to be preferred to the external properties of politeness and elegance. Under these new values, culture came to be a reality close to nature, an alternative to civilization. In Germany, for instance, especially under Herder's influence, interest developed in "folk cultures," and their more natural, less artificially civilized bent. Herder attacked what we might today call "cultural imperialism," the notion that enlightened culture is far above primitive culture. In a blistering passage tying "insult" and "culture" together, he wrote:

> Men of all the quarters of the globe, who have perished over the ages, you have not lived solely to manure the earth with your ashes, so that at the end of time your posterity should be made happy by European culture. The very thought of a superior European culture is a blatant insult to the majesty of Nature.[7]

Here Herder is trying to relativize culture so that it could refer to any social system, not just the supposedly superior one of Europe. Vestiges of Herder's meaning for culture remain today, where it refers to the complex social and symbol systems of "primitive" groups, i.e., those using exclusively oral ways of communicating traditions.

Later in the nineteenth century, as an outcome of the same anti-artificial movement, culture came to signify a process of inner and spiritual development and was connected with art, religion, and personal and family life. Eventually culture was extended to the institutions and practices fostering meaning and values. Culture was what nurtured the imagination, subjectivity, "the individual," fostering inspiration, creativity, and the aesthetic sense. To summarize: In a relatively short period, culture moved from its specific, local meaning of the cultivation of some particular thing, to a word synonymous with the Enlightenment idea of civilization, then to a synonym for nature, and then to signify inner, spiritual development. Though my account of these meanings may seem tedious, awareness of them is important. Vestiges of all these meanings for culture still cling to the word today. During this relatively short period, changes were taking place in Europe that would be much more decisive for our own understanding of culture.

## The Contribution of Marx

The political and social conflicts fostered by nineteenth-century industrial society led to a major transformation of culture as a clearly social concept. Here Marx's insights were crucial. His analysis of civil society helped strip from the abstract term, "civilization," its vague self-importance and give it a specific historical form. Marx showed how the capitalist mode of production had, in turn, produced bourgeois, "civilized" society, with its tendency to name those it exploited as barbarians and semi-barbarians. By exposing the economic base of society, Marx also showed how civilization produced order and refinement for some but disorder and degradation for many others. There was nothing natural or inevitable about any social arrangements. They were all human products which could be examined and rearranged. Of course, such a line of reasoning would quickly lead to the scrutiny of culture itself.

Rejecting "idealist historiography," and its emphasis on overcoming ignorance and superstition by means of reason and knowledge, Marx claimed that knowledge and reason were not enough for understanding social structures. Also needed was the analysis of social arrangements and procedures, an analysis to be developed from the perspectives of varied groups, such as labor and the exploited. Marx's new focus on society had significant consequences. Raymond Williams explains:

> The original notion of "man making his own history" was given a new radical content by this emphasis on "man making himself" through producing his [sic] own means of life. For all its difficulties in detailed demonstration *this was the most important intellectual advance in all modern social thought.* [Emphasis added.] It offered the possibility of overcoming the dichotomy between "society" and "nature," and of discovering new constitutive relationships between "society" and "economy." As...the basic element of the

social process of culture ... [the idea that the human being creates the human world] was a recovery of the
wholeness of history. It inaugurated the decisive inclu-
sion of that material history which had been excluded
from the "so-called history of civilization, which is all a
history of religions and states."[8]

One would expect that this Marxian shift to the human
processes that produced society would have put culture
squarely at the center of social analysis. Instead, and for reasons I will explore in detail in the following chapter, Marx's
followers came to view culture as not concrete or "material"
enough to be studied as one of the bases of society. Until
quite recently, they understood it instead as a realm of ideas,
beliefs, arts, and customs, of "ephemeral" realities which are
determined by the more substantive and basic material processes of life, such as those of the economy. Williams laments
this mistake of not taking culture seriously enough:

Thus the full possibilities of the concept of culture as a
constitutive social process, creating specific and different "ways of life," which could have been remarkably
deepened by the emphasis on a material social process,
were for a long time missed. ... [9]

With culture understood as separated from the deeper forces
that shape social arrangements, its integral connections with
these forces would have to wait till the twentieth century to
be plotted and charted. In the meantime, several areas of
endeavor — art, psychology, and religion — recognized culture's constitutive importance and developed a careful theory
of culture from their own perspectives.

The history of the word "culture" shows, then, that it
did not develop in a straight line of evolution but was at
the mercy of ideological and other social struggles over the
years. Still, remembering its origins as an agricultural term
and its use by privileged classes to name their own superiority gives us an enriched awareness in our own usage of
the word. A person who wants to develop a working theory

of culture will have to be alert to the varied ways the term is used by others who sometimes adopt unwittingly one or other meaning rooted in a particular period. Such alertness is not so easy to maintain. In a course on culture I worked with students to use the word with special care and then noticed that as the semester went on, they tended to use it more and more as a code word that could be applied to almost anything. One of the persons who has done the most to reclaim "culture" as a conceptual tool useful for probing our world of meaning and the way it is produced was Raymond Williams himself. He stressed its character as a signifying system.

## Culture as a Signifying System

The approach to culture I intend to follow in this book is the one laid out in Williams's many writings.[10] The operating definition I use, already cited in chapter 1, is from *The Sociology of Culture*: "Culture is the *signifying system* (emphasis his) through which a social order is communicated, reproduced, experienced and explored."[11] This way of approaching culture emphasizes its active, dynamic character: a signifying system keeping a social order in place. Here we are given points of access for thinking about and exploring the specifics of culture: how a system of signification is communicated, reproduced, experienced. The system can be de-mystified through the scrutiny of these very processes so often overlooked. What is being communicated? Whose vision of reality is it? How did it come to be communicated via this medium?

Though culture communicates a particular social order, that order itself is, in turn, shaped by its system of signifying. A consumerist economic system needs an advertising industry to create markets but then finds the communications idiom of advertising comes to infect the society's own system of political communication.[12] Grasping the material conditions of communications is crucial for understanding any social order, especially how it is kept in place. This fact is only slowly becoming an issue as a new global communications system emerges in our century. Controlled by a handful of wealthy persons, it controls the perceptions of millions.[13] Politics and economics, as social systems for the allocation of power and resources, are now clearly influenced by the material conditions of communications.

Perhaps an illustration will underscore these "dynamic" features of Williams's approach to culture. Many people use the term "culture" to refer to ethnic customs that have survived in a social order other than the one in which they originally developed. Thus they speak of Italian culture among U.S. citizens of Italian descent. Only as a manner of speaking would it be acceptable to talk of "Italian culture" in the United States and to mean styles of cuisine, courtship, family relationships, conflict resolution, attitudes toward alcohol, etc. among persons of Italian ancestry. Although it is common for persons to speak in this way of Polish culture, Irish culture, and many other "cultures," the term used in this sense is more about culinary and other household customs than about culture in the more active way Williams uses the word. Williams does not exclude these traditions from culture, but he focuses on how they are produced, reproduced, and experienced in a particular social order. More simply, Italian culture in Italy is rooted in an economic and political system with a particular history; "Italian culture" in the U.S. refers to certain customs retained even when cut off from the social order found in Italy. In some ways these customs are maintained by the marketing of "Italian" products. There is just as much difference between these customs and Italian culture as there is between American English spoken in Chicago by someone with an Italian surname and the Italian language spoken by a native in Naples. In Williams's use of the term, true Italian culture remains in Italy, because it is only there that the wider social order is communicated, reproduced, experienced, and explored via a signifying system.[14]

## Religion and Culture: The New Situation

Once we view culture as a signifying system, we have a way of connecting religion and culture, since religion is also a signifying system. We are enabled to think at once about both the wider signifying system and the narrower, religious one. A religious system is itself a zone of signification, a culture, but with a difference: religion claims that its meanings and significations are the ultimate ones. Religion's signifying system communicates what might be called "a second-order social system," which stands within another wider social network. The social order of a religion, however, is not an end in itself, even when those directing it treat it as if it were. It exists for some "other" order, in some cases, a future order, which will fulfill the religious quest. For Christians, this order is called "the kingdom of God." Perhaps the reason a revolutionary social movement seems like a religion is that both work for an ideal social order. In general, the secular social order, though far from static, tends toward stasis in the sense of self-maintenance; the religious social order, as an ideal pursued, tends toward radical change, both individual and social, and needs special procedures of maintenance. I recognize that in the actual circumstances of religious and secular life both stasis and the impulse for change are in considerable and more complex tension than my simplification here indicates.

Thus the religious culture is a culture within a wider culture.[15] This perception that the "religious culture" exists within the wider culture seems to be true even when the wider culture *claims to be identical* with the religious system, as in a country with an official state religion. The two systems are never identical, if only because a major goal of the religious culture is fidelity, while for the wider culture it is social harmony and efficiency. The maintaining of a religious signifying system is more intentional and demands more energy than that of the wider culture, partly because the religious realities being signified are not as obvious, not as "natural." Indeed, the wider signifying system's meanings have been termed "second nature,"[16] to describe the natural way culture grows in the soil of the human project. Religion's meanings represent a kind of "third nature."

When groups embrace a particular religious vision of life, their natural tendency is to employ that vision in evaluating various aspects of their own society. On the one hand, the members of any religious group are also part of a wider, non-religious social system, not only speaking its language but employing its own idiosyncratic inflections, embodying that society's deep assumptions about the world, and so forth. On the other hand, when they embrace their religious meanings as ultimate, they stand in a place from which to judge their own society and culture. In the construction of the four Gospels, we can see this process of standing in one culture, the wide, general one of a society, and at the same time, standing within a second religious culture whose meanings critique the first. Writes David Power, "The four Gospels show us how different communities came to tell the story of Jesus Christ by allowing the gospel tradition that they heard to nestle within their wonted ways of perception and challenge their outlook and ways of behavior."[17] All those who hear the religious message of Jesus have to travel the same path, finding ways of sharing their vision of life in narratives that at the same time question the ethical assumptions of a society. As an operative life-force within a people, religion offers new perceptions, new commitments, new patterns of social relations, as well as a series of new freedoms — from fear, from external pressures, even from certain civic laws. Thus, early Christian communities were able to question, though not perhaps as radically as we today would have wished, slavery, marriage customs, military service, the place of women and children in society, and the like.

Tension between the two signifying systems is not new, but the capacity of the wider culture to get its messages across via electronic media is relatively new. Religious leaders find that more and more of those who say they are religious are taking their life's meaning, not from religious understanding, but from the wider culture. As already noted in chapter 1, the religious culture clearly holds its meaning to be ultimate. However, in its character of second nature, the wider culture also demands ultimacy for itself but not so openly. Because of its tacit character, the covert claim has a special power. Not openly made, it is harder to identify and deny. To note these differences and tensions between the two signifying systems in no way implies that features of the wider culture — a tradition of pluralism, for example — cannot enrich the religious culture. On the other hand, the religious culture might have an agenda that the wider culture must not incorporate into law, for example, religious tenets that would, so enacted, destroy pluralism in the wider social order.

The power of electronically amplified and reproduced visuals and sounds has troubled leaders of various religious traditions — including recent popes. These vivid versions of the world sometimes undercut the versions proposed by religious groups. In speaking to those working in various specialties in the field of communications, Pope John Paul II has described in detail the influence of these versions on children and the responsibilities of those who produce them.

> I wish ... to recall briefly what children have a right to expect and to obtain from the communications media. Enchanted by the instruments of social communication and defenseless against the world and adult persons, they are naturally ready to accept whatever is offered to them, whether good or bad.... They are attracted by the "small screen" and by the "large screen"; they follow every gesture represented on them, and they perceive, quicker and better than anyone else, the emotions and sentiments which result.
>
> Like soft wax on which every tiniest pressure leaves a mark, so the child is responsive to every stimulus that plays upon his/her imagination, emotions, instincts, and ideas. Yet the impressions received at this age are the ones destined to penetrate most deeply into the psychology of the human being and to condition, often in a

lasting way, the successive relationship with self, with others, and with the environment. . . .

What then shall be the attitude of responsible Christians and especially of parents and mass media workers conscious of their duties in regard to children? They ought, before all else, to take charge of the human growth of the child; any pretense of maintaining a "neutral" position in its regard and of letting the child grow up in its own way merely disguises a dangerous lack of interest under the appearance of respect for the child's personality.[18]

Though specifically about children, this passage surfaces typical religious alarm about the electronic communication of a world-view.

## The Religious Critique of Culture: The Church as an Example

The *ekklesia* tells a story imagining human possibilities. Centered on Jesus, it is less and less the story that sets life direction for many who call themselves Christians. In response to this dilemma, some, like John Paul II in the passages above and below, are calling for a stance of active resistance to those elements of the wider culture they judge false. Far from a blanket condemnation, such calls propose informed judgment as a form of cultural agency ready to apply norms of human goodness to every proposed rendition of life's meaning.

Secular commentators on culture accept this point. Mark Crispin Miller reminds us that any sweeping dismissal of what he calls "mass culture" dismisses in the same gesture any serious possibility of critique. Serious critique requires nuanced judgment of inadequacies and stupidities as well as appreciation of excellence.

This position [of dismissing mass culture] is — to say the least — questionable. First of all, such a critic tends

to ignore the historical context of mass culture, preferring to groan long and loud for the reinstatement of
some vague code of yore.... For the most part these
grandiose denunciations of mass culture — whether
they derive from Marx or Plato — promote a pleasure-
less view of modern life, whose entertainments have
provided much that is provocative and even beautiful,
and which therefore require the critic to discriminate
among them.[19]

For Miller, the deepest flaw in this dismissive attitude is that
"it actually pre-empts any critical analysis of mass culture by
positing a gross negativity with which all critiques can then
be identified, and so dismissed."

A survey of the speeches and other writings of Pope John
Paul II shows a concern with culture as a system of signification and with encouraging persons to resist what is inhuman
in culture. A few examples from a single series of speeches,
those given in Canada in 1984, illustrate these concerns.
Speaking to educators, he said:

...The radically different cultural expressions and activities of our time, especially those which catch the
popular attention of young people, demand that educators be *open to new cultural influences* and be capable
of interpreting them for young people in the light of the
Christian faith and of Christ's universal command of
love.... Young people today are buffeted in every direction by loud and competing claims upon their attention
and allegiance. From around the world they hear daily
messages of conflict and hostility, of greed and injustice,
of poverty and despair.[20]

A similar concern with cultural critique came up in a homily
to priests:

You have been witnessing, in fact, a *deep-seated process
of change,* one which heralds the appearance of a new
culture, of a new society, but which poses too a number of questions about the meaning of life.... We must,

more than ever, see to it that the voice of Christianity
has a right to be heard in this country, that it might be
freely accepted into the mentality of men and women,
that its witness be expressed, at all levels, in convincing
fashion, so that the developing culture may at the very
least feel challenged by Christian values and take them
into account.[21]

To young people themselves, the Pope had a message just
as explicit, but inviting them to be active in the critique of
culture:

Do not accept a divorce between faith and culture. You
are being called at the present time to a new missionary
effort. . . . In other words, you will develop your culture
with wisdom and prudence, retaining the freedom to
criticize what may be called the "cultural industry," remaining all the while deeply concerned with truth. . . .
Faith will ask culture what values it promotes, what
destiny it offers to life, what place it makes for the
poor and the disinherited with whom the Son of Man
is identified, how it conceives of sharing, forgiveness,
and love.[22]

Such calls to examine culture "with wisdom and prudence,"
while retaining one's right at an early age to critique what is
false, present an important task for religious groups in a time
of electronic communications.[23] Ironically, secular monitors
of communications can offer more hesitations and wisdom
than some religious ones.[24] Implicit in such calls is agreement
with Williams's claim that the conditions of communications
are an important part of the overall material conditions of
life itself, including religious living.

   As valuable as the Pope's ideas here may be, I will show in
chapter 4 how the policy of his pontificate fails to take seriously enough either the possibilities or need for the original
production of religious meaning at all levels of the church.
The cultural resistance proposed by John Paul in these ci-

tations needs to be complemented by new approaches to cultural production in the church itself.

Another side of the religious critique of culture is offered by Gregory Baum, a theologian familiar with the writings of John Paul II. While applauding the Pope's critique of culture from within faith, Baum goes beyond it to note that *all culture, including religion,* has a brokenness and incompleteness needing critique. Baum indicates points of incompleteness in the social system of Roman Catholicism, such as the lack of due process, intolerance of pluralism, and not sufficiently allowing church members, particularly women, to be cultural subjects instead of cultural objects.[25] Examples of this incompleteness could be found in the institutional lives of every other Christian denomination. Baum calls for critique of such elements of incoherence in religious cultures from a point very deep within their own meanings. At the same time, he notes the enrichment of religious groups by movements originating within secular culture, such as the ecological movement. The unfinishedness of any culture as a human project needs to be well understood by religious persons.

## Appreciating the Wider Culture

While needing to critique their religious systems, religious persons must also understand the positive humanizing elements in the secular culture. Critique is not only about what is wrong; full critique makes positive judgments about what is humanly good. Primarily, it seeks to understand how things *work,* to de-mystify processes that have been hidden and not yet invited into the light. Standing squarely within that wider culture, the church, for example, must be able to welcome and applaud every feature of culture fostering the authentic humanization of persons. Because it embraces Jesus' imagination of human possibilities, the church has to rejoice in the ways social systems promote the human project. However, the church is clearly a zone of judgment, assessing both the social order and its signifying system by the criteria of its own meanings, i.e., Jesus' vision of the dignity of persons. A proper formula for making these assessments might be: Quick to affirm what enriches the human project but unafraid to point out what diminishes it. Although in a book like this the positive side of culture is a given, still a reminder of the positive features of culture is in order.

Among positive features of U.S. culture, I would have to mention the following qualities: hospitality that provided a haven for millions of exploited and oppressed people; a tradition of religious and political pluralism; freedom of speech; adventurousness and curiosity, found in a fascination with the unknown; creativity and inventiveness, found in a willingness to try the untried; humor, as found in stories, essays, drama, and films. In the arts, I would have to detail such works of dramaturgy as *Death of a Salesman;* a range of musical forms with varied kinds of appeal; particular novels, poetry, essays; achievements in musical theater; the production of film; and special achievements in the visual and plastic arts. In the field of communications, there are various advancements in telephone, radio, television, sound reproduction, and computers. Among movements culturally enriching to religious groups as well as the wider society, one would have to include the civil rights movement, the Vietnam anti-war movement, and feminism. Still, even here, each of these achievements itself cannot be appreciated fully without critique and without assessment of positive and negative aspects. And as I have already explained, religion, with its own vision of ultimates, provides a source of potential judgment on any human creation.

Perhaps a good description of how this positive and negative judgment might work in practice can be found in the ancient letter to Diognetus, with its depiction of the Christians of that day:

> Christians are not distinguished from the rest of mankind by either country, speech, or customs; the fact is,

they nowhere settle in cities of their own; they use no peculiar language; they cultivate no eccentric mode of life.... Yet while they dwell in both Greek and non-Greek cities, as each one's lot was cast, and conform to the customs of the country in dress, food, and mode of life in general, the whole tenor of their way of living stamps it as worthy of admiration and extraordinary. They reside in their respective countries, but only as aliens. They take part in everything as citizens and put up with everything as foreigners. Every foreign land is their home, and every home a foreign land. (ch. 5)

In a word: what the soul is in the body, that Christians are in the world. The soul is spread through all the members of the body, and the Christians throughout the cities of the world. The soul dwells in the body, but is not part and parcel of the body; so Christians dwell in the world, but are not part and parcel of the world. (ch. 6)[26]

This example should help make clear, then, my position as not claiming that secular culture is bad and the religious sub-system is good. As a human product, any culture has its humanizing aspects, and in fact, only certain features of the two cultures I have been dealing with here clash with each other. Underlying religion's cultural dilemma as I have treated it here is a legitimate concern with *maintenance*. Religious meaning is not self-maintaining. Its perduring over time is an achievement of human intentionality and resulting care. The wider zone of meaning, i.e., culture, with its control of powerful electronic means of storytelling, can tend to gobble up the more narrow one, imperiling its religious vision. Possibly in certain earlier periods, when the wider culture had absorbed more of the values of a religious system, this task of maintaining religious insight did not have to be a central preoccupation of religious groups. The Christian liturgical and catechetical scholar Josef Jungmann, for instance, describes, somewhat fancifully, how such insight was maintained in the late Middle Ages almost by the very ambience of one's life. One brief passage gives the flavor of his essay:

> Apart from the erection of churches that dominated village and city in those times, the landscape breathed holiness from other sources also.... Significant are the many little shrines which everywhere dot valley and mountain. Near the manor house court stands a chapel where devotions were held on an evening or a Sunday afternoon. On wayside paths is found a cross with an image of the crucified.[27]

Jungmann goes on to point out that whatever help was offered by the social milieu of the late Middle Ages in maintaining Christian religious vision, our own situation is very different — and I would add, possibly more similar to that of a Jewish community's effort to maintain its vision in the Europe described here. Even so, in *no* situation is there any automatic maintenance of religious insight. A sign of the vitality of a religious system is the readiness of its adherents to judge other, alternative visions from the position of its own vision and commitments.[28]

The sort of maintenance of meaning I am referring to here is far different from the sort of static maintenance one sometimes finds in overly bureaucratic institutions. Unfortunately the power structures in institutions can maintain themselves by fostering a rote repetition of the traditions of the past, instead of the active questioning and probing characteristic of cultural agents.[29] There is an intentionality of sorts here, but its greatest achievement is muteness and the "chains of command" kind of obedience fostered by the military. In my view, when such bureaucratic maintenance infects religious institutions, the eventual result will be the death of meaning and the gradual fading out of the religious system itself.

In this chapter I have tried to present Raymond Williams's approach to culture, with its particular value of helping us see how meaning is produced and functions in a social order. If culture is, in fact, one of the two or three most complex words in the English language, exploring the history of the word may help us think about the varied uses of the word today, while maintaining for ourselves an active meaning. These distinctions help us understand the relation of religion to culture, and why a religion uses its own meanings as the lens through which culture can be viewed and judged.

In the next chapter, I wish to look at two additional features of culture: first, the reproduction of culture in schools and the problem this poses for religious schools; and second, the question of how culture produces a structure of feeling in particular generations.

## NOTES

1. Here I have followed information found in Raymond Williams's obituary written by Colin MacCabe in the journal Z (April 1988): 59. Of the growing number of biographies of Williams, see, for example, Fred Inglis, *Raymond Williams* (New York: Routledge, 1995).

2. Raymond Williams, *Marxism and Literature* (New York: Oxford University Press, 1977), p. 128. In the next two paragraphs I am summarizing and paraphrasing Williams's ideas in the chapter, "Structures of Feeling," pp. 128–35, of the above work.

3. A helpful explanation for why so many thinkers have avoided looking at culture in its active, productive sense is given by British sociologist Anthony Giddens. He points out that many sociologists, and by extension, those influenced by them, have bracketed out "time" as a concept in their use of functionalism or structuralism, thus giving a snapshot view of society as fixed. Giddens's work tries to restore the flux of ongoing production to the way we view society. See Anthony Giddens, *Central Problems in Social Theory: Action, Structure and Contradiction in Social Analysis* (Berkeley: University of California Press, 1979), pp. 49–65. Michael Schudson makes a similar judgment, but from a different perspective, in "The New Validation of Popular Culture: Sense and Sentimentality in Academia," *Critical Studies in Mass Communication* 4, no. 1 (March 1987): 51–68.

4. Those who make "personal" a synonym of "individual" may have difficulty understanding this point. For a treatment of the central place of the social in the personal, I recommend John Macmurray, *Persons in Relation* (London: Faber and Faber, 1961).

5. Raymond Williams, *Keywords: A Vocabulary of Culture and Society* (New York: Oxford University Press, 1977), p. 76. In another place (*The Sociology of Culture* [New York: Schocken Books, 1982], pp. 10–

12), Williams summarizes three common current meanings for culture: a developed state of mind, as in "a cultured person"; the processes that lead to this state of mind, by which a person is given a chance "to develop some culture"; and the whole way of life of a distinct people or other social group. However, he finds these meanings too limited and static and opts instead for a more dynamic designation of the word, emphasizing that culture is always in process, both in the sense that it is always affecting us but also in the sense that it is always being actively produced.

6. Here I am paraphrasing and summarizing Williams's ideas in two sources: *Marxism and Literature*, pp. 11–20, and *Keywords*, pp. 76–82.

7. This passage is from Herder's *Ideas on the Philosophy of the History of Mankind* (1791) and is cited in Williams, *Keywords*, p. 79.

8. *Marxism and Literature*, p. 19. Paulo Freire offers what I consider a stunning example of helping indigenous people understand culture as a basic way of constructing a human world. By using pictures, he shows unlettered persons how they themselves have constructed a world for themselves and how their sense of beauty and their inventiveness are at the heart of all culture. From this vantage point, Freire invites his hearers to pursue literacy. See Paulo Freire, *Education for Critical Consciousness* (New York: The Seabury Press, 1973), pp. 61–84.

9. Williams, *Marxism and Literature*, p. 19.

10. Williams provides a brief but helpful account of his own evolution in thinking about culture in *Problems in Materialism and Culture* (London: Verso, 1980), pp. 243–44.

11. *Sociology of Culture*, p. 13.

12. For an analysis and contextualizing of this problem, see Adam Gopnik, "A Critic at Large: Read All About It," *New Yorker* (12 December 1994): 84–102. The problem is an international one. See Fintan O'Toole, "Forked Tongues: The Language of Contemporary Politics," *The Furrow* (Ireland) 45, no. 12 (1994): 675–82.

13. See Bagdikian, "The Lords of the Global Village," and Herbert I. Schiller, *Culture Inc.: The Corporate Takeover of Public Expression* (New York: Oxford, 1989). Schiller's book offers a broad overview of the problem but with specific details of how the corporate control of communications works. Related significant works are Richard J. Barnet and John Cavanagh, *Global Dreams: Imperial Corporations and the New World Order* (New York: Simon and Schuster, 1994), and Gilles Lipovetsky, *The Empire of Fashion*, trans. Catherine Porter (Princeton, N.J.: Princeton University Press, 1994).

14. I am aware of the further questions raised by this example, but they are beyond the scope of this book. Is it not possible for culture to be based in language and religion and united by them, but living within different social orders? An example of this phenomenon might be the Armenians when living in the former Soviet Union, with its social order, and

those living in Turkey, with its order. Apparently these people recognize a common language, a common heritage, common customs, etc., but not a common social order. But even in this instance, the ideal sought by many Armenians is a culture that includes a common social order fully under their own control.

Barbara Tuchman's study of fourteenth-century France, *A Distant Mirror* (New York: Ballantine Books, 1987), raises a similar question about an area that had not yet recognized itself as a nation but was moving toward a common language. Another helpful title is John Huizinga's essay, "Patriotism and Nationalism in European History," in his *Men and Ideas* (New York: Meridian Books, 1959), pp. 97–155.

15. For a description of the relation of the two cultures, see Clifford Geertz's essays, "Religion as a Cultural System," and "Ethos, World View, and the Analysis of Sacred Symbols," in *The Interpretation of Cultures* (New York: Basic Books, 1973).

16. This is the helpful term used by Darrell J. Fasching in an essay on the writings of Jacques Ellul, to get at the malleable character of human arrangements. Of course, there is no human nature not marked by culture. There is no first and second nature for humans: humanity means a state characterized by common meanings. See D. J. Fasching, "Theologian of Culture," *Cross Currents* 35, no. 1 (1985): 9–10.

17. David Power, "Liturgy and Culture," *East Asian Pastoral Review* 21, no. 4 (1984): 348–60, at 348.

18. Pope John Paul II, Message for World Communications Day, "Children and the Media," given 27 May 1979, *Origins* 9, no. 3 (7 June 1979): 33–47, at 46. For a secular critique that verifies the Pope's warnings, see David Denby, "Buried Alive: Our Children and the Avalanche of Crud," *New Yorker* (15 July 1996): 48–58.

19. Mark Crispin Miller, *Boxed-In: The Culture of TV* (Evanston, Ill.: Northwestern University Press, 1988), p. 21. The first chapter of this book, "The Hipness unto Death," offers some useful guidelines for critical analysis of TV. Note that Miller's phrase "mass culture" is one I have avoided in this book.

20. "Meeting with Catholic Educators 12 September 1984, St. John the Baptist Basilica, St. John's Newfoundland," *Canadian Catholic Review* (October 1984): 346–47.

21. "To Priests and Seminarians, St. Joseph's Oratory, Montreal," 10 September 1984, ibid., p. 334.

22. "Homily, University of Laval Stadium, Quebec City," 9 September 1984, ibid., p. 325.

23. Among the many speeches John Paul II has made touching on the theme of culture are the following ones of special importance: Address to UNESCO in Paris, 2 June 1980; Autograph Letter on the Foundation of the Pontifical Council for Culture, 20 May 1982; Address to the Pontif-

ical Council for Culture each January, starting in 1983 — to the present; Encyclical Letter *Slavorum Apostoli*, 10 July 1985.

For a fine survey of papal teachings on culture in the wider context of church teaching, see Paul Surlis, "The Relation between Social Justice and Inculturation in the Papal Magisterium," in A. A. Roest Crollius, ed., *Creative Inculturation and the Unity of Faith,* Working Papers on Living Faith and Cultures 8 (Rome: Gregorian University, 1987).

24. See Michael Warren, "Judging the Electronic Communications Media," *The Living Light* 31, no. 2 (Winter 1994–95): 54–64.

25. Gregory Baum, "Faith and Culture," *The Ecumenist* 24, no. 1 (November–December 1985): 9–13. In a similar vein, Brazilian theologian Leonardo Boff has described how the mode of production of a particular society can be reproduced in the structures of the church. In Latin America's dissymmetrical mode of production, the means of production are controlled by a permanent minority who foster the unequal distribution of labor and the unequal distribution of the products of labor. Suggesting that this same pattern has tended to be adopted by the Latin American church brought down on Boff the ire of the church bureaucracy. See Leonardo Boff, "Theological Characteristics of a Grassroots Church," in S. Torres and J. Eagleson, eds., *The Challenge of Basic Christian Communities* (Maryknoll, N.Y.: Orbis, 1981), pp. 124–44.

26. Cited in J. A. Kleist, ed., *The Ancient Christian Writers,* no. 6. (New York: Newman Press, 1948), pp. 138–40.

27. Josef Jungmann, "Religious Education in Late Medieval Times," in Gerard S. Sloyan, ed., *Shaping the Christian Message* (New York: Macmillan, 1958), pp. 38–62. Jungmann's essay, which seems to idealize somewhat the positive Christian tone of the period, must be seen in the context of his wider corpus of writings, which gives much attention to the problem of the communication of faith in modern times. The essay cited here establishes the distance between the two periods.

28. David Power's "Liturgy and Culture" is a good statement of this position.

29. I have described this process in churches in "Catechesis and the Captive Audiences," chapter 3 of *Faith, Culture, and the Worshiping Community.*

*Chapter 3*

# CULTURAL REPRODUCTION AMONG THE YOUNG

In this chapter I seek to get at the notion of cultural reproduction by examining the creation among the young of a "structure of feeling," particularly by means of schooling. This one aspect of cultural reproduction can illustrate how a culture can successfully imprint (i.e., reproduce) a social order in the consciousness of particular people. One of the best descriptions I have found of the end result of this complex process is offered by John Kavanaugh, who begins his analysis with the following scenario:

> The man is a blue collar worker. He tells the story of his nine-year-old daughter. She said that the only thing she really wanted for Christmas was a pair of Vidal Sassoon jeans. He explained to her that they really weren't wealthy enough to afford $40.00 jeans. Maybe Levis would do. "Forget it," she said. "If I can't have what I want, I don't want anything."
>
> The man said that they saved up and got her the Sassoon jeans for Christmas. "But you know," he mused, "she judges the others in her class on what kind of designer jeans they have. They form cliques based on their clothes. It's their way of being somebody, being acceptable, being 'in.' "[1]

Kavanaugh goes on to probe the significance of what is happening to this girl and how it has happened. Explaining the agricultural etymology of the word "culture," he points out that culture "feeds" us the human meanings cultivated by a particular society. Since it feeds and sustains us, culture has an urgency in our lives analogous to food itself; it is a basic human need. Culture feeds us in ways that feel "ultimate" to us and that seem fulfilling. Culture should itself be formed in the image and likeness of human personhood, whereas in fact it can do the opposite and form persons in some other image and likeness. It could reduce personhood to a single dimension, i.e., as consumers, and then work to form persons in that image. But whatever image of the person it communicates to us, it does so in a total and dominating way.

This background helps explain what is happening to the nine-year-old at Christmas. Her identity, at least in part, depends on the purchased object. Her own sense of her social grouping is based on commercial imagery and on gaining acceptance by copying commercial images. Sadly, her relationship with her parents, at least in this matter, is fixated at the level of commercial images. She has evaluated their love by the norm of their ability to help her measure up to commercial imagery. Her "affect" toward her parents is marked by sullenness and misunderstanding. Kavanaugh asks how all this happened and then proceeds to outline the forces which have shaped her spirit for her lifetime.

Before she went to school, if her home was at all average, she had spent as much time before the TV set as she would later spend in all her classes, including those for a first university degree. On TV she found human beings fulfilled and made happy through products. Good judgment was depicted as the ability to select the right products to buy. Most of these products are assigned names designed to give them ultimate human value. "Merit" is a cigarette, as is "True." "Life" is a cereal for breakfast. "Joy" and "Happiness" are fragrances for the body. Unlike the human values they are drawn from, these names are all of products available for a price. In some of this imagery, relationships are portrayed as disposable while the product is not: "My wife got the house, but I got the Sony."

When Kavanaugh is finished reciting these aspects of the commodity culture that have affected this little girl, all surprise at her reactions to her parents' lack of Christmas cash has evaporated. The culture has reproduced itself in her, and one now sees how it happened. Though the girl's anxiety was rooted in what her peers in school would think of her, she learned her basic lessons apart from the school, through assumptions about reality communicated by advertising. This example of cultural reproduction will be important to keep in mind in the following pages as I examine the particular kind of reproduction that schools themselves foster.

So far I have claimed that the church is meant to function as a zone of ultimacy from which the wider culture can be judged, though to be sure, it will not succeed in that task in any automatic way. As a construct of the social order communicated by culture, the school, on the other hand, tends to reproduce rather than judge the culture of a particular society. Schools provide a helpful example of how cultural production and reproduction can function almost unnoticed. At the same time, of course, they possess a latent capability of enabling the young to see, judge, and, if necessary, contest aspects of culture. As my example from Kavanaugh's analysis shows, I am not implying that schools are the dominant or the most successful means of cultural reproduction in a society. Parenting probably deserves that honor. Compared to schools, military training is a much more successful system of social reproduction for the way it gives the young, not just a training in how to kill and follow orders, but in an explicit political ideology that often lasts into old age. I doubt one can understand the "culture of violence" in the United States without exploring its relationship to the militarization of the young. Still, here I have elected to study the school as especially germane to my purposes.

The theory of social reproduction is complex, with most treatments of it carefully nuanced. Essentially, it is not a theory about schools alone but about how many social institutions succeed in imposing their agenda as necessary and unquestioned. It holds that each aspect of a social order can be understood as a mode of production, i.e., as a way of producing some particular system (a political or economic structure; or some structure of communications, such as one that communicates the "news") which, at the same time, produces the way of thinking needed by that social order. When that way of thinking is in place, then the order itself is established and accepted. Once functioning, the social order seeks *to reproduce* the conditions of its own existence, and by a variety of means.

For example, a political structure needs intellectuals whose prime task is to make reasonable and acceptable the dominant political meanings and practices, thus helping them spread.[2] A political structure also needs to find ways of presenting the interests and ideas of those in charge, not as arbitrary but as a necessary and even natural part of the wider social order. It is here that schooling works as an important social and political force for reproducing a society's political agenda. In Michael Young's succinct statement:

> Those in positions of power will attempt to define what is to be taken as knowledge, how accessible to different groups any knowledge is, and what are the accepted relationships between knowledge areas and those who have access to them and make them available.[3]

If the school can succeed in appearing as an impartial and neutral communicator of a particular social order's benefits,[4] then it will be able to promote inequality itself in the name of fairness and objectivity. Henry Giroux explains that social agenda functions in schools through

> a set of material practices through which teachers and students live out their daily experiences. Ideology has a material existence in the rituals, routines, and social practices that both structure and mediate the day-to-day workings of schools. This material aspect of ideology is clearly seen, for example, in the architecture of school buildings, with their separate rooms, offices, and recreational areas — each positing and reinforcing an aspect of the social division of labor. Space is arranged differently for the administrative staff, teachers, secretaries, and students within the school building.[5]

A growing literature has taken pains to explain in detail how the school's overt and covert curriculum succeeds in repro-, ducing a society's fundamental power relationships, i.e., with some persons dominant and others subordinate. What such descriptions sketch is not a conspiracy at all,[6] but rather a not-to-be-overlooked aspect of schooling that passes on a society's signifying system and, along with it, its social order. However, should a particular school contest the social or political order, say on religious grounds, and be seen to do so successfully, the school could expect trouble, even possibly to the point of political assassinations.[7]

## Schools and the Selective Tradition

One of the ways a school succeeds in reproducing a social order is through passing on a particular tradition as *the* tradition. Tradition, as I use it here, is not some entity from the past, now existing as the "surviving past." Tradition viewed that way is somewhat dead, and if alive, only so because of our attention. It has no hold over our present. As I intend it here, tradition is a powerful and active shaping force in the present. It is "the most evident expression of the dominant and hegemonic pressures and limits" of the present social system.[8] Tradition pressures us to think a certain way and sets the limits of alternative ways of thinking. If we see tradition in this way, we have access to its vitality in its continuing influence on ourselves. At the same time our naming tradition this way allows us to question its inevitability.

Within a particular social system, what most often happens is that a specific version of tradition is selected and presented as *the tradition,* exactly because it embodies certain meanings and practices while neglecting others. Literary traditions, for example, have a way of excluding and thus silencing certain voices such as those of working-class writers.[9] Because those lacking full access to society's benefits would be more critical of the social order, their writings tend not to be accepted as part of the literary canon. As a version of reality, a tradition is selected for the way it represents important aspects of the contemporary social and cultural organization and because these aspects are important for maintaining the continued dominance of a particular social class. When presented as *the* tradition, that is, as the way things are and have always been, such a selective version of reality has great power. *It is a version of the past meant to ratify the present with an illusory sense of continuity.* In Williams's words,

> What we have to see is not just "a tradition" but a *selective tradition:* an intentionally selective version of a shaping past and a pre-shaped present, which is then powerfully operative in the process of social and cultural definition and identification.[10]

Though tradition is commonly understood as a weak reality, a nostalgic option, this other, often unnamed but active form of tradition is a powerful ratification of a contemporary order.

For all its power, the selective tradition is also vulnerable to data not fitting its version of reality. For this reason it is quick to "discard whole areas of significance, or reinterpret or dilute them, or convert them into forms which support or at least do not contradict the really important elements of the current hegemony."[11] Certain ideas are declared outdated; and the contributions of whole segments of a people are dismissed as insignificant. On the other hand, the most powerful work of exposing the selectivity of the dominant tradition can be done through the revisionist study of history, because it offers a chance to see more clearly where things come from, or to reinterpret or even contradict the current versions.[12] In Williams's view, "This struggle for and against selective traditions is understandably a major part of all contemporary cultural activity."[13] While schools tend to reproduce the dominant meaning systems of a social order via processes like the selective tradition, they need not do so. Critical teaching can offer alternatives.

The literature dealing with cultural reproduction in schools both questions "the selective tradition" and seeks to expand educators' understanding of their actual work in culture, with an eye to encouraging a more active critique of meaning systems. This literature is especially fascinating for the nuanced way it describes and analyzes the effects on consciousness and behavior of various procedures used in schools. Many writers show cultural reproduction as not automatic but often contested by students. Yet, ironically, the very contestation is, in turn, absorbed by the reproduction process itself.[14] This literature deserves close study by all associated with schools.

If understanding cultural reproduction opens up the possibility of fostering a critical consciousness in the young in schools in general, it should have special significance for those teaching in religious schools.[15] A critical consciousness is rooted in cultural agency, since it assumes one has a right to be involved in examining and questioning aspects of the signifying system. As I have already pointed out, a person committed to a religious vision tends to examine reality from the perspective of that vision, and so one might expect in religious schools a particularly sharp angle of religiously based critical analysis. Still, critical thinking as a form of cultural agency can be fostered by any teacher offering students specific skills needed for interpreting and contesting the selective tradition and other forms of cultural production. These are the skills of cultural analysis.

Michael Apple reminds teachers that they are members of wider groups than those in their school, that they have commitments to realities other than the school, and that those commitments may open up for them and enable them to open for their students alternative points of view. As Apple says:

> ...It should be clear that educators are not simply members of a community of other school people... [but] of a larger collectivity whose values provide the fundamental framework for their thought and action. This fact means that any *critical* [emphasis added] act in an educational sense is by necessity an act that is critical of the dominant normative structure of the larger

society. Educational criticism, hence, becomes cultural, political, and economic criticism as well.[16]

Apple's point is that educators have the potential ability to question the dominant social structures and thus disrupt mindless reproduction. When they do so, it is because they recognize education itself as moral and political activity.

The potential of educators in schools to engage in the cultural activity of "critical demystification" is unlimited. For students, the processes by which communication is produced and "works" seem to be entirely "natural," taken for granted, and closed to reflection. In the classic Marxist sense, such students are alienated: a humanly produced entity is viewed as necessary and unquestionable. Education can put these forms of communication into students' hands in more than one sense. Williams claims that critical demystification should be an accepted part of a normal education but in a "lab" context:

> The critical demystification has indeed to continue, but always in association with practice: regular practice, as part of a normal education, in this transforming process itself; practice in the production of alternative "images" of the "same event"; practice in processes of basic editing and the making of sequences; practice, following this, in direct autonomous composition.[17]

The project of critical demystification in both church and school — and the scope of the problems facing both areas of demystification — is clarified by Williams's explanation of "structure of feeling."

## Culture and the Structure of Feeling

"Structure of feeling" is a concept developed by Raymond Williams to describe attitudinal shifts and emphases that emerge from particular cultures in particular generations. For him, it is "a cultural hypothesis,"[18] that is, a conceptual tool for disclosing an aspect of cultural reality. In his various writings, starting with *The Long Revolution* (1961), Williams again and again describes this idea from subtle and varied points of view, always careful to keep it open, suggestive, and almost vague. As a hypothesis, this concept is valuable for the way it helps us recognize culture's shaping of *affect,* and for its connections with similar terms used by other cultural analysts.

Williams uses the word "structure" to suggest the definite and firm side of what he is describing, while holding on to its subtle, less tangible character. Structure of feeling refers to characteristic ways of seeing and judging that emerge from the social and cultural patterns experienced by particular generations. In one of his earliest treatments, he claims that a particular structure of feeling is not taught by the dominant generation to the rising generation. In fact, it does not appear to have come "from" anywhere. "A new generation responds in its own ways to the unique world it is inheriting...feeling its whole life in certain ways differently and shaping its creative response into a new structure of feeling."[19] This somewhat mystified way of dealing with the genesis of the structure of feeling seems to belie Williams's own stress on how culture is produced.

In later writing, he is more specific about the possible origins of shifts in the structure of feeling. He locates these origins in the efforts of one generation to induct the new generation into its social system. The older generation hands on fixed forms which they themselves have lived and which have shaped their own social consciousness. However, the new generation finds these fixed forms no longer precisely fit their own practical experience. The young have what Williams calls their own "practical consciousness," which they are actually living and practicing. In Williams's words:

> There are experiences to which the fixed forms do not speak at all, which indeed they do not recognize.... Practical consciousness is almost always different from official consciousness...for practical consciousness is what is actually being lived, and not only what it is

thought is being lived. Yet the actual alternative to the received and produced fixed forms is not silence....It is a kind of feeling and thinking which is indeed social and material, but each in an embryonic phase before it can become fully articulate and defined exchange.[20]

An example of the emergence of a new structure of feeling in our own time might be what is sometimes called a new "visual culture," where many people are growing up immersed in visual images in a way persons born before TV were not. The production, mass reproduction, and accessibility of visual material seem to be eroding the capacity of many people to gain perspective on their social world.[21] The dominance of images as the way in which many persons take in information about the world tends to reduce language and thought codes to the dimensions of visuals. During the Reagan and Bush election campaigns in the 1980s, alarm over the diminishment of political discourse and the effective control of perception via televisual images provided an indication of a significant shift in the nation's structure of feeling.

As social theorist Stanley Aronowitz has noted, "the truncated imagination now appears natural." He notes that recent psychological research discloses

a tendency towards narrowing of perception, imitative patterns of child's play, disruptions of concept formation among school children, the visual character of thought, and the increasing difficulties experienced by children in performing abstract and logical functions. The research suggests a correlation of television watching (and consumption of mass culture in general) to a tendency towards literalness in thought. Here, the merging of thought with object seems to have become the new universal of human consciousness.[22]

Aronowitz finds these research findings verified among his own college-level students who "seem unable to penetrate beyond the surfaces of things to reach down to those as-

pects of the object that may not be visible to the senses."[23]
When students tend to be so overwhelmed by the factuality
of the world that they are unable to move to concepts which
may controvert appearances, teachers face a new structure of
feeling requiring educational correctives. What is true of the
young when actively examining ideas in classrooms seems all
the more characteristic of persons at all levels of society. Immersed in images that shape their affect, they are less and
less able to think about how these images work. Through
"structure of feeling," Williams is seeking to describe particular qualities of social experience and relationships which
characterize a generation or a period. The specific qualitative
changes involved in the evolution of such social experience
are, from the beginning, rooted in *social* experience rather
than in what many like to call "personal" experience. This
point is important to keep in mind, because with Williams's
stress on the emergence of a structure of feeling in a new
generation, one might tend to overlook his equal stress on its
emergence out of particular social conditions. Had Williams
read Paul Fussell's *Wartime: Understanding and Behavior in
the Second World War*,[24] he would have found a detailed
example of a socially produced structure of feeling repli-
cated during World War II by all social institutions so as
to have long-term effects in a nation's consciousness and its
militaristic institutions.

In perhaps his most specific description of this concept,
Williams admits the term he has picked is difficult and then
defends the choice:

> The term is difficult, but "feeling" is chosen to em-
> phasize a distinction from more formal concepts of
> "world-view" or "ideology.... " We are talking about
> characteristic elements of impulse, restraint, and tone;
> specifically affective elements of consciousness and re-
> lationships: not feeling against thought, but thought
> as felt and feeling as thought: practical conscious-
> ness of a present kind, in a living and interrelating
> continuity.[25]

Williams seems to hold that no single master factor shapes a particular structure of feeling. Yet the task of the cultural analyst is to search out elements in culture and their connectedness that may work together to shape a particular structure of feeling. Important clues to structure of feeling can be found in art, literature, film, and television, where often occur the first indications that a new structure is forming. In *The Country and the City*, Williams himself carefully traces in British literature of the later eighteenth and nineteenth centuries shifts in the structure of feeling toward rural life and industrialization. Many came to have a nostalgic longing for the idealized "simple life" of the country, but thereby ignoring the causes in industrialization that led to many being moved off the land. Williams shows how this affectively based notion came to inhabit poetry and fiction. These perceptual shifts did not materialize out of thin air but were, bit by bit, fostered by writers offering a particular rendition of reality.

One can see why Williams, examining culture as a living signifying system, would have to develop a hypothesis like structure of feeling in order to help explain how whole generations can come to see and name reality in the particular ways they do. It is worth noting that a fair number of his examples of structures of feeling, like the one explored in *The Country and the City*, are negative, showing how a population can come to embrace particular illusions and misunderstandings.

I, myself, have found the "structure of feeling" notion helpful for examining shifts in consciousness in our time and for noting the ways the production of culture has influenced the production of affect. Since religious forms also propose an "affect," or habits of the heart, to those who embrace these forms, the whole question of structure of feeling and how it is shaped will be a keen interest to religious groups. Also, Williams's emphasis on the structure of feeling in the rising generation helps us note shifts in the way the young encounter and name their life in society. Williams's concerns here are similar to those of Aronowitz and many

others who seek to chart the affective aspects of the functioning of culture,[26] what Robert N. Bellah calls the "habits
of the heart."[27]

Bellah and his associates invited persons from varied
walks of life to talk about their sense of themselves and their
life commitments. They found that most of these persons
lacked a language with which to speak about their connections to any transcendent reality, not even to the wider
society. "Insofar as [these persons]...are limited to a language of radical individual autonomy, as many of them are,
they cannot think about themselves or others except as arbitrary centers of volition. They cannot express the fullness
of being that is actually theirs."[28] Bellah's team found that
most of the persons they interviewed took their sense of their
life's significance from external signs of success and from an
inner sense of being adjusted or comfortable. The following
description of their interviewees comes close to Williams's
structure of feeling concept:

> The two traditions of individualism [out of which most
> people in the U.S. operate] offer us only the cost-benefit
> analysis of external success and the intuition of feeling
> inwardly more or less free, comfortable, and authentic
> on which to ground our self-approval. Ideas of the self's
> inner expansion reveal nothing of the shape moral char-
> acter should take, the limits it should respect, and the
> community it should serve.[29]

Bellah ascribes these attitudes to individualism. Williams
would want to go further and probe the specific cultural
products: essays, novels, plays, festivals, television, films,
portrayals of reality via news reports, and social policies by
means of which such an approach to reality evolved.

Another concept that might be related as a kind of theoretical "cousin" to Williams's structure of feeling is Pierre
Bourdieu's "habitus," used to describe the internalization of
a society's programme.[30] Like the nine-year-old girl of John
Kavanaugh's scenario, one comes to embody ways of knowing, valuing, and relating to the world so that they become

embedded in one's "natural" patterns of perceiving and acting. These ways of being, though in a sense subjective, are
actually quite objectively produced by the social conditions
of particular classes.[31] Bourdieu explores how structures can
be patterned into a person's whole way of being — without
being consciously accessible to the person. In his words:

> The principles em-bodied in [the habitus]... are placed
> beyond the grasp of consciousness, and hence cannot be
> touched by voluntary deliberate transformation, cannot
> even be made explicit; nothing seems more ineffable,
> more incommunicable, more inimitable, and, therefore,
> more precious, than the values given body, *made* body
> by the transubstantiation achieved by the hidden per-
> suasion of an implicit pedagogy, capable of instilling
> a whole cosmology, an ethic, a metaphysics, a politi-
> cal philosophy, through injunctions as insignificant as
> "stand up straight" as "don't hold your knife in your
> hand."[32]

Bourdieu seems deterministic in describing the stubbornness
of these dispositions and their inaccessibility to thought. I
presume he intends to say, much as Paulo Freire does, that
the taken-for-granted is *ordinarily* not questioned, except
through careful steps that disclose how it is socially constructed. The sort of cultural agency needed to map those
steps will involve hard work, because the way modern communications functions is complex and the way its meaning
comes to reside in us is subtle. Bourdieu's writings, like those
of Williams, represent just such an attempt to disclose the
social construction of culture.[33]

The following chapters on production and on images will
offer educators, both church and non-church related, some
clues as to how they can work with critical demystification
through cultural analysis. Education as a moral endeavor,
that is, as an effort to foster awareness of the behavioral implications of ways of seeing and perceiving, calls educators
to a somewhat new task: discerning how people actually approach their "world" and fostering a critical awareness of

just these ways of perceiving. This book has sprung from my own attempts to face this task.

# NOTES

1. John Kavanaugh, "Capitalist Culture as a Religious and Educational Formation System," *Religious Education* 78, no. 1 (Winter 1983): 50–60, at 50. I summarize and paraphrase many sections of this essay.

2. Here I am following an early section of Michael Apple, "Reproduction, Contestation, and Curriculum: An Essay in Self-Criticism," *Interchange* 12, nos. 2–3 (1981): 27–47.

3. Michael F. D. Young, "An Approach to the Study of Curricula as Socially Organized Knowledge," in M. F. D. Young, ed., *Knowledge and Control* (London: Collier-Macmillan, 1971), p. 32. An overview of the thinking behind this literature is Henry A. Giroux, "Theories of Reproduction and Resistance in the New Sociology of Education: A Critical Analysis," *Harvard Educational Review* 53, no. 3 (1985): 257–93.

4. An example might be the way the U.S. utilities spent millions of dollars each year in the 1980s constructing school curriculum or at least curricular materials on "the environment," all filled with conviction about the necessity of nuclear power. One utility provided week-long all-expenses-paid workshops for almost a thousand teachers in its region and boasted that it had "influenced 1,552,320 students." See Kirk Johnson, "Schools Test the Environmental Waters," *New York Times* (21 November 1989), pp. B1, B6.

5. Giroux, "Theories of Reproduction and Resistance," p. 264. Giroux here is setting forth one of Althusser's understandings of ideology.

6. Again Apple puts the matter well: "Curricular and teaching practices are never the result of 'mere' imposition; nor are they generated out of a conspiracy to, say, reproduce the conditions of inequality in a society.... Exactly the opposite is the case... [and] they will be guided by an urge to help and make things better... " ("Reproduction, Contestation," p. 39).

7. Though my statement here may seem like a silly exaggeration, a most interesting example of just such a contestation on religious grounds is Charles J. Beirne, SJ, "Jesuit Education for Justice: The Colegio in El Salvador, 1968–84," *Harvard Educational Review* 55, no. 1 (1985): 1–19.

8. Raymond Williams, *Marxism and Literature* (New York: Oxford University Press, 1977), p. 115.

9. This matter is a recurring theme in many of Williams's writings, though his most systematic recovery of these voices is *Culture and Society*

*1780–1950* (New York: Columbia University Press, 1983). Feminist scholarship has, for the past two decades, been hard at work recovering these silenced voices and giving them a hearing.

10. *Marxism and Literature,* p. 115.

11. Ibid., p. 116.

12. A telling example is Frances Fitzgerald's study of U.S. history textbooks and their patterns of painting history as the work of charismatic men in key leadership positions, rather than the result of effective checks and balances in a political process that allowed a certain amount of dissent. Even when not tolerated, dissent and intellectual conflict were features of many developments in U.S. history. See Frances Fitzgerald, "Onwards and Upwards with the Arts: History Textbooks," *New Yorker,* 26 February, 5 March, and 12 March 1979. These essays were published that same year in book form. Aspects of the "forgotten tradition" would include the place in U.S. history of religious dissent, dissent and non-cooperations with militarism, and conscientious objection.

13. *Marxism and Literature,* p. 117. The selective tradition became a national controversy in the 1980s, partly because of Allan Bloom's *The Closing of the American Mind* (New York: Simon and Schuster, 1987), which sought to maintain a particular tradition of letters as normative. Among hundreds of essays appearing since Bloom's book, see the following, which alludes to the selective tradition in its very title: Henry Louis Gates, Jr., "Whose Canon Is It Anyway?" *New York Times Book Review* (26 February 1989): 1, 44–45.

14. On this last point, see Apple, "Reproduction, Contestation," especially for his description of Paul Willis's study, *Learning to Labour.* Also, Paul Willis and Philip Corrigan, "Orders of Experience: The Differences of Working Class Cultural Forms," *Social Text* 7 (1983): 85–103, esp. pp. 98ff.

Michael Apple, of the University of Wisconsin, is the person who has shed most light for me on cultural reproduction via education. Some of his other writings are: *Ideology and Curriculum* (Boston: Routledge and Kegan Paul, 1979); *Education and Power* (Boston: Routledge and Kegan Paul, 1982); "Class, Culture and the State in Educational Interventions," in Robert Everhard, ed., *The Predominant Orthodoxy* (New York: Ballinger Press, 1983); "Work, Gender, and Teaching," *Teachers College Record* 84, no. 3 (1983): 611–28; "The Hidden Curriculum and the Nature of Conflict," in William J. Pinar, ed., *Curriculum Theorizing: The Reconceptualists* (Berkeley: McCutcheon, 1975), pp. 36–53; Michael Apple and Thomas Brady, "Toward Increasing the Potency of Student Rights Claims: Advocacy-Oriented Policy Recommendations," in V. Hanbrich and M. Apple, eds., *Schooling and the Rights of Children* (Berkeley: McCutcheon, 1975), pp. 198–207; "Analyzing Determinations: Under-

standing and Evaluating the Production of Social Outcomes in Schools,"
*Curriculum Inquiry* 10, no. 1 (1980): 55–76.

15. I have already dealt with aspects of this question in *Youth, Gospel,
Liberation* (New York: Don Bosco Multimedia, 1994).

16. "The Hidden Curriculum," p. 90.

17. Raymond Williams, "Means of Communication as Means of Production," in *Problems in Materialism and Culture* (London: Verso, 1980),
p. 62.

18. *Marxism and Literature,* p. 132.

19. *The Long Revolution,* p. 49.

20. *Marxism and Literature,* pp. 130–31, passim. Other social thinkers
have struggled with the same phenomena Williams tried to get at through
"structure of feeling." In his essay "The Problem of Generations," Karl
Mannheim describes how the young can come into contact with culture
in a new, fresh way, with more social distance from the "accumulated heritage" than the previous generation. Such contact gives rise to fresh insight
and a selection among what is acceptable or not in culture. Mannheim's
ideas here complement Williams's. Karl Mannheim, "The Problem of Generations," in *Essays on the Sociology of Knowledge* (London: Routledge
and Kegan Paul, 1972), esp. pp. 291–95. If one assumes, based on internal evidence, that this essay was written around 1952 or earlier, one can
ask whether Mannheim, had he been writing in the 1990s, would have
dealt at length with the problem of electronically communicated imagery.

21. This is the point of David Denby's *New Yorker* essay, "The Buried
Child," cited above.

22. Stanley Aronowitz, "Mass Culture and Critical Pedagogy," chap-
ter 3 of Stanley Aronowitz and Henry Giroux, *Education under Siege*
(Granby, Mass.: Bergin and Garvey, 1985), pp. 47–55, at 47–48. Neil
Postman has dealt with this problem in many writings, among them,
"Engaging Students in the Great Conversation," *Phi Delta Kappan* (Jan-
uary 1983): 311–16. Particularly important are Postman's *Teaching as a
Conserving Activity* (New York: Delta, 1979), and *Amusing Ourselves to
Death: Public Discourse in the Age of Show Business* (New York: Viking
Penguin, 1985).

23. Aronowitz, "Mass Culture," p. 49.

24. Paul Fussell, *Wartime* (New York: Oxford University Press, 1989).

25. *Marxism and Literature,* pp. 131–32.

26. I am aware of a vast literature charting cultural shifts and "structures of feeling" in Williams's sense. Christopher Lasch, Richard Sennett,
Philip Rieff, Alisdair MacIntyre, and Robert N. Bellah are just a few of
the men who have worked to chart the origin and progression of specific
shifts in the thinking and acting of contemporary persons. Almost all feminist writers are working in a similar way in the history of ideas. Here,
because of my concern with electronic communications, I give special at-

tention to those who have described the connection of these cultural shifts with electronic media. Here again, there is a vast literature. A good place to begin in this literature might be with the writings of Walter Ong of St. Louis University, and an introductory essay might be, "Literacy and Orality in Our Times," *Journal of Communication* (Winter 1980): 197–204. I also recommend the writings of George Gerbner, Stuart Ewen, Todd Gitlin, Robert M. Liebert, and, as already noted, the recent writings of Neil Postman.

27. Those familiar with the book produced by Bellah and his associates know that the expression "habits of the heart" was actually coined by Alexis de Tocqueville in the 1830s, though Bellah has given it new life. See Robert N. Bellah et al., *Habits of the Heart: Individualism and Commitment in American Life* (Berkeley: University of California Press, 1985), p. viii.

Initially I thought Clifford Geertz's use of "moods" might be another of these affective terms, but closer study showed he does not account for social causes the way Williams does with "structure of feeling." See Clifford Geertz, *The Interpretation of Cultures* (New York: Basic Books, 1973), pp. 96–98.

28. Bellah et al., *Habits of the Heart,* p. 81.

29. Ibid., p. 79.

30. I, myself, have tried to set out Bourdieu's understanding of habitus in: "The Worshiping Assembly: Possible Zone of Contestation," *Worship* 63, no. 1 (1989): 2–16; and "Life Structure or the Material Conditions of Living: An Ecclesial Task," *New Theology Review* 8, no. 4 (1995): 26–47.

31. Bourdieu's entire book *Distinction: A Social Critique of the Judgment of Taste* (Cambridge, Mass.: Harvard University Press, 1984) is about this point, which, for this reader, he demonstrates in a convincing way. For a more succinct statement of his position, see pp. 100–101, where he examines "the economic conditions of the production of the dispositions demanded by the economy" (p. 101).

32. Pierre Bourdieu, *Outline of a Theory of Practice* (Cambridge: Cambridge University Press, 1977), p. 94, as cited in Giroux, "Theories of Reproduction and Resistance," p. 270.

33. I have tried to combine the perspectives of Williams and Bourdieu in "Cultural Coding in the Young: The On-going Dilemma," *Listening* 25, no. 1 (Winter 1990): 47–60.

# Chapter 4

# CULTURAL PRODUCTION AS AN AVENUE TO CULTURAL ANALYSIS

In the previous chapters, we have seen that culture, as a signifying system producing and reproducing a social order, exercises powerful influence in the lives of all. The signifying power of electronically reproduced images influences the imagination, especially that of children and young people. Perhaps Stanley Aronowitz names accurately the extent of this influence:

> In the last half of the twentieth century, the degree to which mass audience culture has colonized the social space available to the ordinary person for reading, discussions, and critical thought must be counted as the major event of social history in our time. Television, film, and photography, far from making culture democratic, have fostered the wide dissemination of industrialized entertainment so that the capacity of persons to produce their own culture in the widest meaning of the term has become restricted.[1]

In this situation, the churches are concerned about ways of imagining the meaning of life that counter their own religious vision. For the churches and others, such as parents, concerned for a humanizing vision of life, the work of maintaining their own distinctive vision of reality involves finding forms of cultural agency. These include becoming aware of the various versions of reality being offered us, especially through electronic narratives, becoming adept at judging these narratives, and proposing our own alternative versions and narratives. A definition of culture as an active process of signifying, such as the one Williams proposes, invites cultural agency because it invites us to investigate how the process works.

So far I have often adverted to the importance of cultural production for helping us see how culture actually works. In this chapter, I seek to explain cultural production in greater detail, using as examples the production of technology, the production of specific artifacts such as music and toys, and finally, the production of religious meaning. The processes by which a signifying system itself is produced, so easily taken for granted and overlooked, are in fact concrete and visible. Because what is unnamed is unseen, I seek to name and highlight cultural production as observable procedures open to our analysis. Understanding specific points in the production process can make us aware of culture in its concrete steps of coming into being. It can give culture a human face.

Every photo is someone's framing and rendition of reality; every TV scenario is someone's version of what life is all about;[2] every written news story is someone's interpretation of an event. Even further, someone has edited the news story and awarded it a particular position on a page; the TV scenario has been directed and recorded from various angles and then screened for its acceptability by business and advertising personnel; the photo taken by one person has been made available to us by many, including some who may have altered it in fundamental ways. Understanding such processes lays the foundation for the sort of agency I call cultural analysis. As human beings we are not to be mute and powerless in the face of activities meant to influence us. The parent, for example, who begets and nurtures a child should be able to speak to the shaping of a child's affections that takes place through children's toys. The parent's vocation is to be more than a passive consumer of such artifacts, unable to think about their short and long-term consequences.

My aim at this point is to deal with the production of culture at first from a broad angle and then from a progressively
more specific one. The broad angle is the story of how cultural production came to be regarded as of less importance
for social analysis than other forms of production in society.
My hope is that this story will help attune the reader to the
importance of cultural production as much as it has helped
this writer.

## Marx and the Subsequent Ignoring of Cultural Production

Unfortunately, analysis of the production of signification has
not always been regarded as worthwhile, let alone possible. Raymond Williams, as a revisionist Marxist scholar, has
described the sequence of events that eventually led to the
neglect of cultural production as an area of inquiry. Though
the story of how this happened may seem obscure and irrel-
evant at first, it highlights important aspects of culture as a
signifying system and the way attention to the process of production can expose that system. In Williams's account, the
sequence of neglect was unintentionally initiated by Marx
himself.

Especially in his famous Preface to *The German Ideology,*
co-authored in 1846 with Friedrich Engels, Marx attacked
a notion common in the German idealism of his day, that
ideas are primary causes in the world. Instead, he proposed
that ideas are not so much causes as effects, outcomes of the
material conditions of people's lives. The reality that people
live creates what is in their heads, rather than the thoughts in
their heads creating the material conditions of life. In Marx's
Preface he offers a parable to illustrate this conviction:

> Once upon a time an honest fellow had the idea that
> men were drowned in water only because they were
> possessed with the idea of gravity. If they were to knock
> this idea out of their heads, say by stating it to be a

superstition, a religious idea, they would be sublimely proof against any danger from water. (*GI*, 2)[3]

Gravity exists as an idea because it is a physical reality first. The idea of gravity is a sort of second-level reality based on its prior physical actuality. Here Marx's intention is to affirm the prior place in reality of the concrete conditions of life, though in doing so his very example seems to name ideas as insubstantial. In a later passage, probably co-written by both Marx and Engels, once more the language used seems to name ideas as illusions:

> We do not set out from what men [*sic*] say, imagine, conceive, nor from men as narrated, thought of, imagined, conceived, in order to arrive at men in the flesh. We set out from real, active men, and on the basis of their real life-process we demonstrate the development of the ideological reflexes and echoes of this life-process. The phantoms formed in the human brain are also, necessarily, sublimates of their material life-process, which is empirically verifiable and bound to material premises. Morality, religion, metaphysics, all the rest of ideology and their corresponding forms of consciousness, thus no longer retain the semblance of independence. (*GI*, 14)[4]

Marx makes his point effectively: let us pay close attention, not so much to what people say about their lives as to what "real life processes" they actually live "in the flesh." By refusing to approach reality from the side of idealized accounts people give of existence, Marx (and Engels) was making an important contribution to thought: reality should be approached the other way around, starting with the specific habits and ways people live out their everyday lives. It was appropriate that ideas be deprived of their illusory independence from the actual process of life and that they be reconnected with what he called the material conditions of life.[5]

Unfortunately, Marx's insights about these matters were

themselves distorted by his own rhetoric which seemed to put down ideas as illusory and insubstantial. In his effort to stress the influence of social conditions upon ideas, he gave the impression that ideas were secondary to social processes, whereas his intent was the opposite, to show their close connection. This is how Williams puts the problem.

> The language of "reflexes," "echoes," "phantoms," and "sublimates" [used to refer to ideas and consciousness], is simplistic, and has in repetition been disastrous.... The emphasis on consciousness as inseparable from conscious existence, and then on conscious existence as inseparable from material social processes [which was Marx's point], is in effect lost in the use of this deliberately degrading vocabulary.[6]

Williams insists that Marx, his rhetorical emphases notwithstanding, from the very beginning saw consciousness as part of the human, material social process, so that the products of consciousness, that is, ideas, were so much a part of social process that they themselves must be included among the material products and conditions of life. The production of meaning was central to Marx's concerns.

When Marx and Engels's convictions were later systematized by others, these others tended to repeat the separation of idea from actuality — but from the opposite direction. They made the material processes of life so fundamental in their social theories that ideas then tended to become "mere ideas," not fully integral to the materiality of life. Once such a separation becomes accepted, consciousness is relegated to a secondary status, that of a lesser reality. Worse still, culture and the processes of communication come to be not included among the "material processes of life." When that happens, cultural analysis ceases to be seen as an integral part of social analysis. In fact, however, no account of the social is adequate without taking close account of the production and communication of meaning, that is, culture.

Williams rebuts this refusal to see ideas as integral in social process in a passage worthy of being cited at length:

... Consciousness and its products are always, though in variable forms, parts of the material social process itself: whether as what Marx called the necessary element of "imagination" in the labor process; or as the necessary conditions of associated labor, in language and in practical ideas of relationship; or, which is so often and significantly forgotten, in the real processes — all of them physical and material, most of them manifestly so — which are masked and idealized as "consciousness and its products" but which, when seen without illusions, are themselves necessarily social material activities. What is in fact idealized, in the ordinary reductive view, is "thinking" or "imagining. . . . " *What this version of Marxism especially overlooks is that "thinking" and "imagining" are from the beginning social processes . . . and that they become accessible only in unarguably physical and material ways* [emphasis added]: in voices, in sounds made by instruments, in penned or printed writing, in arranged pigments on canvas or plaster, in worked marble or stone. . . . The "practical process" of the "development of men" necessarily includes them from the beginning, and as more than the technical means for some quite separate "thinking" and "imagining."[7]

The analysis of the particular material ways by which thinking and imagining are socially shaped is thus an important part of any adequate understanding of society. More simply put, if the TV is on in the average U.S. home about eight hours a day, and if, between the ages of 6 and 18, the average child spends 16,000 hours in front of a TV set, these facts spell out material conditions of the lives of many in our society. The analysis of signification and, more broadly, of culture centers not on abstractions but on material processes involved in signification. Williams makes this same point in a later passage: " . . . The practical links between 'ideas' and 'theories' and the 'production of real life' are all [to be found] in this material social process of sig-

nification itself."[8] This is a point too long overlooked by
educators quick to recognize the value of their own work
of communicating culture but slow to see either the implicit
messages of educational institutions or the explicit power of
electronic media.

It has been Williams's own work that has helped reclaim
the study of cultural production from the secondary, "su-
perstructural," status awarded it in earlier Marxist theory
and brought it to its present position as "a constitutive social process, creating specific and different 'ways of life.' "[9]
Williams's contribution has been to halt the abstraction of
culture by refusing to let it be separated from material social
life. I claim this contribution has significance for religious
persons. Whatever social processes create specific and different ways of life also shape people's spirituality and should
have intense interest for those concerned with the religious
dimensions of life.

## Language as the Seminal "Product" in Cultural Production

What are the products in cultural production? This question
is one Williams asks in many places and from varied perspectives in his written work over a period of thirty years,
offering ideas complementing one another but never brought
together in a single theoretical work. His basic answer is that
since culture is a signifying system, its products are commu-
nicative ones which function as usable signs. These signs do
not simply develop by themselves; they are socially produced,
and, once they are operative, a person is born into them, so-
cialized in them. As persons, we do not find "language" as
one static entity and "society" as another; instead we have
an active social language as one of the most basic products
of a society. Neither is this social language a mere reflection or expression of material reality. *Language is the vehicle
by which material social reality is grasped.* Language is the
stream, words are the canoe, and thought is the person in the

canoe who can go only where the stream goes and either goes in that canoe (or some other floating conveyance) or does not go at all. As Williams has written, "Language . . . as practical consciousness is saturated by and saturates all social activity, including productive activity."[10] Feminists have understood this matter so well that they have worked to change sexist language as one key step in countering sexist thinking. If men want to change the way they act towards women, they must change the way they talk about women, including possibly their syntax.

This conviction explains Williams's lifelong work to trace the historical development of ideas as seen in the changing use of language. His little book, *Keywords,* is an example of cultural analysis of the social forces that shaped the meaning of certain words so that they came to signify what the social system needed them to signify. Cultural analysis via the analysis of words and word clusters has been carried forward by Peggy Rosenthal in her *Words and Values: Some Leading Words and Where They Lead Us,*[11] a work inspired in part by Williams's own *Keywords.* Also used by Robert Bellah and his associates in *Habits of the Heart,* this kind of analysis provides a basic tool for understanding how signifying systems work.[12] As Freire helped us understand, an important form of cultural agency involves being able to notice and then question the way the world is named. Re-naming is a form of radical action.

## Rescuing Production from Determinism

Williams's concern with cultural production goes beyond a concern with words, as important as that concern is. If words as means of communication can be studied for the way their meaning is produced, so too can all other forms of communication. Means of communication are themselves means of production, from the simplest forms of language to the most advanced forms of communications technology. All these forms deserve scrutiny from human beings born to be

agents. However, many tend to exclude forms of communication from critical thought and instead treat them as if they
fell magically from the heavens. Williams has given special
attention to the problem of what he calls "technological determinism," an assumption that technology is inevitable and
can only be accepted.

An example of his attempt to question unspoken assumptions about communications technology is found in his little
book on television. Examining nine "typical" statements
about the way television has altered our world, he then uses
each to expose a kind of intellectual passivity in the way we
think about communications technology. I paraphrase them
here as an example of how one person works at exposing
technological determinism:

1. Once television resulted from scientific and technical
   expertise, its effectiveness in communicating news and
   entertainment became so great that it changed all earlier
   news and entertainment media.

2. Once television resulted from scientific and technical expertise, its power in communications became so massive
   that it changed both our institutions and patterns of
   social relationships.

3. Once television resulted from scientific and technical
   expertise, its characteristics as an electronic means of
   communication so radically shifted our perceptions of
   reality that our relationships with one another and with
   the world underwent a dramatic change.

4. Once television resulted from scientific and technical expertise, its ability to communicate and entertain then
   combined with other newly developed technologies,
   such as new forms of transportation, to change the
   kinds of societies we now live in.

5. Once television resulted from scientific and technical expertise, its ability to communicate and entertain had
   unexpected consequences, not only by decreasing the

importance of other news and entertainment channels but by shifting key aspects of social and cultural life, including family life-patterns.

6. Once created by scientific and technical cunning, television then received the investments that made possible its special social contribution of providing centralized entertainment and the centralized shaping of opinion and styles of behavior.

7. Its possibilities developed by scientific and technical research, television came to be promoted as an exciting component of a domestic consumer economy: a machine needed in every home.

8. Emerging from scientific and technical creativity, the actual uses of television fostered in a heightened degree the cultural and psychological passivity that has long existed as a tendency in society.

9. Once developed by scientific and technical research, television came to be exploited to serve "a new kind of large-scale and complex but atomized society."[13]

The first five statements present the technology as almost accidental, with no reason given why a particular invention was, in fact, pursued and developed.[14] We have a sort of "invention without intention." Once developed, however, its effects were inevitable: "application without intention." Notice that all five statements are in the passive voice, the voice that masks agency. In each statement we have a "double passive": the invention "happened" and the outcome "happened." Such a way of stating reality incorporates a common, orthodox view of social change, which Williams calls "technological determinism." Technicians pursuing their own scientific instincts happen to develop a new technical invention, which in turn "makes" the modern world. Williams exposes here a false notion of agency, which goes hand in glove with a mind-set unwilling to question how things came about.

The second set of opinions, numbers 6–9, appears less
deterministic, in the sense that the invention, after it "happens," is then put to particular uses. Each statement implies, however, that inevitable social conditions determined
these uses, rather than some group's intention. In the end,
then, both sets of statements are deterministic because both
remove technology from intentionality. Restoring intentionality to the story of technology restores the human faces
behind particular decisions about the uses of technology.
A technology's uses are as much a human product as the
technology itself.

As socially and materially produced and reproduced, all
means of communication call for analysis.[15] Some analytic
questions: How was a particular communications technology, say radio or television, developed? In whose interests
was it developed? In the popular use that came to be made
of that technology, what alternative uses were proscribed
and how? For example, could radio have been developed
as a basically interactive medium instead of in its present
form? In asking such questions, Williams rejects Marshall
McLuhan's naïve acceptance of communications technology
as a "given." Enthusiastic talk about the "global village"
created by TV betrays a blindness to the medium's potential for manipulation and helps overlook the human
decisions that have shaped our world.[16] It does not deal
with whose information is being shared in the global village nor with the distortions in the way one part of the
village might be represented to another part. In a medium
like television, needing large sums of money to produce dra-
matized material and relatively tiny sums to reproduce it,
will those who control the money needed for production,
and who then sell televised material for export, come to exercise a kind of cultural imperialism on societies with less
capital?

In the 1980s a handful of giant private organizations began to dominate the world's mass media. Their goal was to
control by the end of the century most of the world's important newspapers, magazines, books, broadcast stations,

movies, recordings, and video-cassettes. The possibilities of misusing such control of what are sometimes called the "culture industries" should make all thoughtful people pause:

> The lords of the global village have their own political agenda. All resist economic changes that do not support their own financial interests. Together, they exert a homogenizing power over ideas, culture and commerce that affects populations larger than any in history. Neither Caesar not Hitler, Franklin Roosevelt nor any Pope, has commanded as much power to shape the information on which so many people depend to make decisions about everything from whom to vote for to what to eat.[17]

This matter deserves the attention of all concerned with a humanizing cultural environment, and, in fact, it is being closely studied by some engaged in communications theory.[18] My conviction is that ordinary people can come to ask these and similar questions as a normal way of inquiring about the world in which they live.

## Critical Demystification

This last sentence makes a claim about the possibility of posing critical questions about the production of signification. A skeptical reader will ask, Is it in fact possible? My response is that, yes, it is possible but *not easily possible*. The work of enabling this possibility will be, especially in the beginning, a work of careful education. As an example, for over forty years, many in the West have been immersed in television images, and the time is overdue for them to be able to think about how those images "work." Only recently have scholars like Stuart Ewen done the kind of writing that shares the skills needed to understand and then to question the production and use of images.[19] Religious groups like churches and synagogues might be expected to be in the forefront of this work, since their agenda and the agenda of the television marketeers are often so disparate. Living within a religious community that embraces its own distinctive vision of reality as a way of life lays an indispensable foundation for the kinds of critical questions I have in mind.

In a time of electronic communication, there are two different skills involved in dealing with the technology of production. One is skill in actually using the technical means of production. A person with such skill could use it as a functionary with no concern for the uses to which that skill is being put. This kind of skill tends to be out of the reach of most in the population. Another is skill in understanding the general functioning of the technical means of communication and in critiquing them. This is a skill of *critical demystification,* and like literacy itself, it can be made widely available. As a skill, critical demystification asks and pursues answers to a series of questions about the production of culture via electronic communication: How does the technology work? Who has access to it and who is excluded? Whose voices and views are presented and whose excluded? Who controls access and the views presented? What alternative sources of communication are available to those excluded?

Among these questions the key to critical demystification is the one that asks: Who wants me to see what I am seeing from the angle I am being allowed to see it, and why? This seemingly obvious question, once asked and pursued in its implications, opens up for scrutiny an immense area of human agency in electronic communications — the agency of those who produce the meanings being communicated. This question asked, the agency of the questioner can now come into play and could conceivably provide a countervailing kind of agency, especially through educational or organizational work.[20] When feminists name the men producing TV commercials showing mindless women failing at ordinary household chores, some women will turn off the set and even refuse to purchase the products advertised. In 1989, the Home Box Office cable network produced a half-hour video laying out for children the way toy advertisers manipulate them with false and incomplete claims. Entitled "Buy Me That," it shows the possibilities of demystification at early ages.

Williams uses editing as an example of a technical process that, when understood well, facilitates the posing of critical questions about electronic communications. He points out how the edited image gives the illusion of being an action transmitted directly:

> We hear a man speaking with his own voice, or he "appears" as himself: on the screen. Yet what is actually being communicated, after the normal processes of editing, is a mode in which the primary physical resources have been — usually in... hidden ways (the edited-out words cannot be heard) — transformed by further intermediate labor, in which the primary communicative means have become material with which and on which another communicator [i.e., the editor] works.[21]

A person can be taught to understand how this process works and even how a technical matter like the positioning of a camera becomes a crucial element in signification itself.[22] In recording a confrontation between demonstrators and police, one will see what happened from a different social perspective if the camera is located behind the police than if it is located behind the demonstrators or in some impartial location.

Williams claims that the skill of critical demystification is best taught in conjunction with practice in the use of the technology. This practice, which should be part of a normal education, involves efforts to produce alternative images of the same event from different viewpoints; practice in the process of basic editing and in devising sequences of images. That this sort of practice toward demystification is not unknown is shown in the following description of an eighteen-minute video and study guide made by students at the Schomburg Satellite Academy in New York City during the 1991–92 Persian Gulf confrontation and war:

> The video ["Through Our Eyes"], which explores Iraq's take-over of Kuwait and the dispatch of U.S. troops to Saudi Arabia, [is] accompanied by a student-written study guide linking the Gulf War with on-going social and political issues.... Last September, students wanted to understand why the U.S. had sent troops to the Persian Gulf. To find out, they studied maps, interviewed experts about the region, attended antiwar rallies, and surveyed the opinions of other students. They shot film, taped, and edited. The result, completed before the war began, makes a strong statement opposing U.S. military intervention.[23]

Such practice is not so much toward production skill as toward a fuller understanding of how various processes work. To use a literacy analogy, one comes to fuller literacy in attempting to work in various genres and thereby appreciating how meaning is created in those genres.

## Examining Cultural Products at Points of Consumption and Production

I would hope readers have now come to the conviction that it is not enough to examine a cultural product only at its point of consumption; it must also be examined at its various points of production. By "the point of consumption," I refer to the moment we encounter a cultural product. We see a TV program or watch a film or hear a song for the first or the fifteenth time or read an account in a newspaper. The product is there before us, already produced. Many people "consume" such products "as is," responding that they did or did not like it or did or did not agree with it, and that is the end of it. A step beyond such naïve consumption is the ability to critique the product for distortions of the truth or from the perspective of some commitment, say a commitment to nonviolence, to the rights of women, or to a religious perspective. The ability to "see what one sees" or to reflect on what one reads or to examine what one hears remains a key critical ability. Yet such an ability is necessary but insufficient for the kind of cultural analysis I am trying to get at in this book.

For a fuller understanding of cultural products one must also examine them at the various points of their production. These are the points in a process that has eventually produced what one encounters at the point of consumption. Let me illustrate what such points might be in a newspaper account of some event in another country, say, a massacre of peasants by the military in Guatemala. The report offers me information about the event. If I merely read the article and consume its information as fact, I have failed to consider adequately enough what is involved in this cultural product, and further, I may have participated in a quasi-fraud.[24] The news report represents some person's viewpoint. And I can ask a critical question, the most basic question of cultural analysis: Who wants me to understand what happened in this way? Related questions might be: Is the writer someone whose work I know and can trust in its factualness? Is s/he located in the place where what is being reported happened, or is the report second, third, or fourth-hand, since some reporters may want to be based in the more affluent cities of the region they are covering and such cities do not exist in Guatemala? Are there any aspects of the report I would want to know more about or question?

Though some of these questions hint at an awareness of points in the production process, someone with a more explicit awareness would ask another series of questions. This report appears in a newspaper. What is the editorial policy of the paper and how might it affect this report? What has been the quality of its reporting about Central America? What has been the character of its editorial opinion of events in that region? Who owns the newspaper and what interests — economic, political, social, etc. — does this ownership represent? What are the possibilities that the report itself has been edited to suit an editor's point of view or even to fit into the space available in a particular column of print? What corporations or groups provide advertising revenue for this newspaper and what control over editorial policy do they exert? Has the country in which the event took place developed its own news dissemination apparatus, so that any news from its sources can be expected to be influenced somewhat by its political agenda?

Implied in these questions is a distinction between an immediate production process and an intermediate one. The immediate production process involves the steps that led more or less directly to the appearance of the report in this paper: a reporter (with his or her own agenda) sent to a country to gather information, the filing of a report with a news desk, the editing of the report, and its appearance within the context of a particular page layout. However, there is also an *intermediate* production process: the ownership of a newspaper, national and international agencies that gather and disseminate "news," advertisers whose payments become part of the salaries of reporters and editorial staff, a readership that reads in particular ways, and so forth. Finally, there is even a remote production process, which involves the history of news gathering and of newspapers themselves, including the political or financial controls to which they have been subject. The analysis of the processes of production is not complete without this historical dimension.

Someone has told me the questions raised here are certain to cause migraine. I am not suggesting one think through all these questions in reading a news story, but rather that they represent an overall frame of reference needed for our times. Is this sort of thinking too much to expect of ordinary persons? Perhaps. What is more certain is that a habit of mind enabling one to think about the chain of the production of meaning will not happen by accident. Intentional efforts needed to inform others about this aspect of production have hardly begun. If being able to think this way is a factor in bringing adult questions to the information and perspective presented to us via media, the work of fostering such thinking must begin.[25]

The possibilities of these efforts are heightened if we consider a single recent shift in popular consciousness: awareness of the production of chemicals and their influence on the environment. Influenced by health-related information available in the 1970s and 80s, many persons have come to think actively about the chain of production involved in ordinary drinking water or in the food they eat. Many now know it is a simplification to think of water and food as automatically "natural" and healthy. Information about the quantities of toxic chemicals in the air and ground have led them to consider and question the specific conditions of the various steps in the growing and processing of food and in the providing of drinking water. After decades of simply assuming the food and water in their homes to be pure and healthy, they no longer take these matters for granted. In a similar way, people may come to question cultural production and its influences.

## The Production of "Popular" Music and Toys

The habit of mind similar to that needed to understand the production of news stories could be applied to popular music. The questions asked would go beyond whether the music or the words-and-music pleased me. One would have to ask about the agenda of the composer, of the lyricist, of the singer. When a woman is hired to sing a song written by a man, there arises a potential issue of sexual politics. When a woman sings a song expressing a male's sexual fantasy as if it were her own, thinking women *and* men need to be alerted to potential distortions or reality. But the song in its final form on disk or tape is more than the work of composer and singer. Many hands have been involved in its production: arrangers, orchestrators, various musicians, a variety of persons with a variety of technical skills. What are their interests in the production of this song? Should the song distort the relation between the sexes, one can ask about the gender of those involved in the wider production process;

should the song be aimed at the youth market, one can ask about the ages of the producers. What profits, financial and extra-financial, can they be expected to reap from the production and marketing of this particular song? How exactly is the production done? Who decided that this particular song would be produced? Is there worthy music being composed that never gets produced and marketed? Why? Who was in charge of the marketing? How much "showcasing" was involved in the marketing? While copyrights protect the "rights" of producers of this material, what protections are there for its consumers? These are only some of the questions that can be asked when we move toward a critical examination of cultural production.

If I were to try to systematize some of these questions by means of a diagram, I might do so by means of the various frames that could be used to examine a particular song. It is possible to look at a particular song within three sequential, increasingly comprehensive, frames. Each frame has its own questions that seek to examine how its elements function. The first or innermost frame is that of the song itself. Most persons who listen to songs never go beyond this key frame, but many never think very deeply even about this frame. Questions regarding this inner frame would include the following: Does the song have lyrics or not? If so, who sings them, a man, a woman, a group, or what combination of these? If the song has a story or narrative, what is it? Can we retell that story in our own words to see its meaning and implications? In what way does the music underscore (or fail to underscore) the narrative? What instruments are involved and how do they underscore the song's message? If the song does not have a narrative, what meaning does it have? What mood does it create, what message does it offer?

The second frame is that of the song's production. This frame shows us that the song did not get from the songwriter to the listener by a magical process. If we apply here our earlier consideration about the production of culture itself, we get a broader sense of what really happens in modern forms of the production of meaning. The production of most cultural products, in this case a song, is part of a more complex chain of production. Self-expression of the song's composer is but a part of this chain, which itself is more similar to the production of some manufactured item than to the mythicized self-expression of some individual artist. The production of another cultural artifact — toys — offers perhaps a closer model of the steps in production than does the idea of the free self-expression of a lone artist. However, self-expression and freedom of speech seem to be the issue favored by those who object to questioning the marketing of any cultural product. I claim that freedom of expression is not the same as freedom of production. Freedom of production is under the control of many social agencies. If a manufactured object is found to be defective or dangerous — again, children's toys might be an example — the producers are required by law to take the defective product off the market and correct the defect before being able to re-market it. My own question is whether the original self-expression of an artist should be automatically extended to the mechanical reproduction and the marketing of the work.[26]

This second frame of the song's production, then, encompasses the smaller, inner frame of the song itself and looks in at it from the point of view of the song's production. Some questions asked in this frame might be: Is the writer/composer a man or a woman? Is the singer a man or a woman? If the writer is a man and the singer is a woman, then whose point of view does it present, a woman's or a man's? What is the message/agenda of the composer? What are the names of the others who have been involved in this song's production: those who orchestrated, performed, engineered the sound, designed the label and jacket, directed the overall production? Who directed the marketing of this song? These questions get behind the simplification of naming one single person, the main performer, as an "artist," thereby ignoring the chorus of persons that had a hand in the complex production process. What is their gender, what is their age? What might be expected to be the age or gender of the persons this song will appeal to?

The third frame is the frame of value. From this vantage point we can ask other sets of questions allowing us to make judgments about the song from outside the two frames of the song's meaning and production. Focusing on this frame highlights that we have a right to make judgments and assessments about any artifact presented to us. Though each frame represents a kind of agency in thinking about the song, this one is more clearly evaluative and thus involves a special form of agency. What might be some of these sets of questions? For example, one could ask a series of questions from a religious perspective. Does the song have a religious message, and if so, how do we judge it? Does it have any message that merits judgment from a religious point of view? From another angle, one could ask how those who hear the song might be expected to respond to it or what influence it might have on those persons. For example, how might a child of ten, say a young girl, respond to it, or a boy of fifteen, or a married adult? Does the song address agendas teens are struggling with, and if so, do we judge that the song distorts the issues or sheds light on them? The answers to these latter questions are not simple, because multiple layers of meaning having multiple effects, some contradictory, lie encoded in music.

## Frame Analysis of "Young Turks"

Frame analysis, as I have tried to describe it here, can be refined and adapted to many kinds of cultural products. An approach through "frames" allows us to see, if not the whole picture, then at least more of the picture. Frames allow us to see an ever-expanding perspective or an ever-wider angle. The value of a frames approach is its attempt to get behind the complex matter of cultural production and disassemble some of its components for better analysis. Perhaps its value will be clearer if I illustrate it with an analysis of a particular song, "Young Turks," by Rod Stewart. Not a "new" or recent song, I use it to demonstrate an approach that might

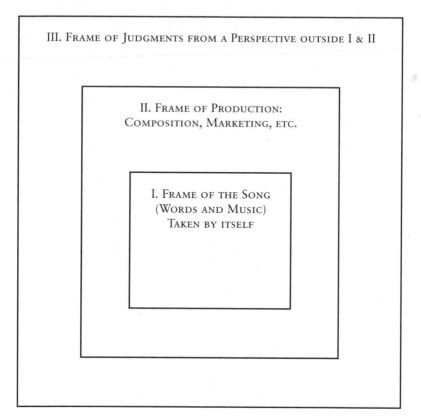

be applied to songs of the reader's choice, underscoring here at the outset that songs are meant to be listened to as music first before subjecting them to this sort of analysis.

"Young Turks" is a narrative song with a driving beat underscoring the urgency of the narrative action. The back-up guitar highlights the action described in the narrative, as does the refrain, with its insistent and even compelling message. The refrain calls for young people to embrace their own freedom because time is on their side. The refrain then goes on to advocate three points of resistance to the oppression from older people by not allowing oneself to be put down or pushed around or even allowing one's point of view to be changed.

When I first heard the song I was involved in teaching

young people how to resist oppression and speak out on key social issues. The refrain caught my attention for its message of resistance — until I heard the third point of resistance, about *not ever* letting one's point of view be changed. Shifting one's point of view may be essential at various points in one's life, and is itself a sign of open flexibility and youthfulness, even in the aged. In a refrain advocating resistance, here was a suggestion to be questioned. It led me to study the song carefully for its message about liberation. Here I summarize the narrative in my own words, warning readers that my own version seems somewhat silly when cut off from its tight elucidation by the music. Readers would do best by listening to the actual song.

In the narrative, regularly punctuated by the refrain, Billy and Patti are dissatisfied with their lives. Billy decides anything would be better than the life he is living and leaves home with a dollar in his jeans and "a head full of dreams." Meanwhile Patti, just turned seventeen, packs her bags, writes a note to her mother, and tearfully kisses her younger sister farewell. Cuddled close to each other and excited, the young couple drives all night, convinced they are taking their one chance at life while young enough to be unafraid. After all, life is so brief that if you can't decide what action to take it will slip away through your fingers like sand.

They drive toward the coast because that is where paradise seems nearest. There they find a tiny apartment "jumping every night of the week" and their expected happiness. Billy has his ears pierced and drives his pickup "like a lunatic." Finally Billy writes Patti's parents a letter attempting an explanation. He apologizes that things "had to turn out this way." He says he couldn't talk because nobody was listening: that was the reason they just ran away. The final line of the narrative explains that Patti has become the mother of a "ten-pound baby boy."

This narrative has a strong message about a line of action taken by two young people and their reasons for it. The context of the narrative is to justify this line of action. The following is another rendition of the narrative and action as faithful to the sense of the song and in as objective a manner as has been possible for me.

Young people should be free and make their own decisions, without being put down or pushed around by older persons. In the light of that position, Billy leaves home with basically no money but convinced by his dreams he could live a better life. Patti also leaves home, not quite as sanguinely as Billy but with greater forethought. She packs more than one bag, leaves a written explanation for her mother, and emotionally bids her sister goodbye. At this Patti falls silent in the narrative and, in a sense, disappears, until its very last line. Except for that line, all initiative seems to lie with Billy.

They go to the coast driving excitedly all night in one another's arms. Apparently Patti's more methodical preparation to leave and her emotional ties to her family are behind her now in her excitement. Or could it be the excitement is felt more by Billy than Patti? However, the narrative credits both with this excitement, which also has a "blissful" side to it. Time is running out for them and so they are decisive in their action. At the coast they find an apartment where they can be happily in each other's arms but also where they party every night. Billy especially embraces his new-found freedom, by piercing his ears and driving his pickup truck with the abandon of a madman.

Billy now writes Patti's parents, complementing Patti's letter to her mother. We know nothing of Billy's own home or his affect toward his parents. They never come into the narrative. Possibly Patti's parents are more significant to him. We are not told. We *are* told of Billy's apology, which he then takes back in his explanation that the action they took was not a choice; it was inevitable; it simply had to be. The reason for its inevitably was that no explanations or even dialogue about what they did was possible because nobody was listening. In the end Patti takes action of a sort by giving birth to a ten-pound baby boy. This frame one rendition of the narrative is incomplete without the underscoring offered by the music, something available only through a recording.

In frame two, we name all the persons we can find who have been part of the production of the song. The narrative is about young people of each gender, depicting the permissions they gave themselves. Since the young people are fictional, these permissions are, of course, those *imagined for* Billy and Patti by the song's composer, Rod Stewart, a man at least twice Patti's age at the time of the song's production. We do not know Billy's exact age.

The man-to-woman ratio of those associated with this particular song, including the album in which it appears, is ten to one. Males have imagined, composed, written, scored, orchestrated, performed, recorded, and marketed this album — and designed the album jacket.

In frame three, we go back and make some judgments about the song and its production. We may rate the orchestration, with its combination of guitar and synthesizer, punctuated with a powerful beat, to have good musical quality, which effectively underscores the sense of the narrative. In addition, Rod Stewart's somewhat rasping voice has a distinctive quality to it, a sort of unpolished pleasantness.

The message of the narrative, however, calls forth another question. A man near forty, who has earned a considerable fortune from sales of his songs to the young, is now offering them a narrative of what their life could be like. In the narrative are embedded permissions to do what the two characters did. At its center, this narrative celebrates the judgment of a young man who left home ill-prepared for the journey, let alone the life he was embarking on. Without ties to family or friends, this young man's primary connection is with his lover, Patti, and *her* connections. Her family ties notwithstanding, he takes Patti far from her source of support to a small apartment where they share bliss and fun. His own personal freedom is symbolized — and celebrated — by pierced ears and wild driving. In the end, Patti gives birth to a very large male child. At this point a person hearing the song might reflect back and inquire whether there was some disregard for Patti and her unborn child hidden in Billy's driving habits.

On further reflection, other questions bubble to the surface. What is it like for a girl of seventeen to give birth to a ten-pound baby? What is it like for a girl so young to care for an infant, especially when cut off from those who might support her in that task? What is the rate of child abuse for young mothers her age in her circumstances? What sort of parenting style might one expect from the Billy of the Rod Stewart narrative, this bejewelled free spirit careening around in his pickup with his dollar? What would it be like to care for an infant in an apartment "jumping every night of the week"? Or would that life-style have changed with the arrival of the child?

Further questions might be able to reveal the truth of Billy's claim that he could not communicate because "nobody was listening." Does Billy seem like a good communicator, given Mr. Stewart's own selection of detail for us? Do we find we trust his judgment? If not, can we believe his claim?

How would teen women view Patti's situation if, say, they were her close friends, but were so far away they could not support her in any of the various ways young women help one another? How would they feel if they were in her situation? Would they want to be in a city far away from home, living with someone like Billy? What sort of stability would they expect of Billy in a love relationship?

Some final questions about the song's initiator, Rod Stewart: Do we trust the young people we love to Mr. Stewart's imagination of what sort of freedom is healthy for young people? Is Stewart a friend of youth or is he one of the problems youth need to be wary of? When Billy and Patti begin to buy expensive child-care items like a crib or stroller, what percentage of their income would they have to lay out? On the other hand, if Mr. Stewart himself had a child, what sort of living space would the child be in and what sort of assistance could he afford to purchase for himself and his lover/ wife? In Mr. Stewart's universe, would there have been as much rejoicing if Patti had given birth to a ten-pound baby girl? As these questions suggest, there may be lurking in this song issues of ageism, classism, and sexism that begin to emerge only after serious questioning.

To return to an earlier question: Are such questions about the music they hear possible for young people? My own answer is again tentative. Young people might reject some of the judgments implied in these questions, but they can and should be challenged to think about who imagines the world for them, what their gender and socio-economic status are, and whether their messages are to be trusted. I have yet to meet a young person — or a person of any age for that matter — willing to admit being influenced by audio and visual stimuli. Many, however, will admit to alarm about what such stimuli do to their younger sisters and brothers. Unable to recognize any danger to themselves, they become engaged when invited to think about the rising generation. In human generativity there is an inclination to want to protect those younger. Here I have not been proposing a formulaic answer to the question of being able to think about music. Instead I offer clues, possibilities, and avenues of action, and invite readers to learn how to speak with young people about these matters. The goal is to remind them of humanizing criteria to use in making judgments about what we hear.

## Analysis of Production and Consumption: Children's Toys

A related approach to examining cultural production looks at the following: (1) the point of consumption, a necessary but insufficient angle from which to examine a particular cultural product; (2) the immediate points of production; (3) the intermediate points in the production process; and finally, (4) the history of the medium in question or the technology involved in it or of the institutions that support it. The more broadly cultural analysis examines the processes by which a particular product came to be, the more adequate the analysis.

Such analysis will not be complete, however, unless one

takes notice of a complicating factor in consumerist societies: so much communication is directed by a marketing industry whose major work is the *production of consumption,* that is, the orchestration of desire towards greater consumption. Here, obviously, I am using consumption in a different sense from my use above to name the point at which a person encounters a communications product. Here consumption means *purchasing* and bringing into one's home. Still, those who would do cultural analysis well must keep in mind how much all communications production is under the economic control of the production and orchestration of consumption.[27] Market analysts are busy discerning how to unlock human needs and desires. In a 1974 report to advertisers, market analyst Arnold Mitchell predicted "consumer values" in the 1990s, as follows:

> The central problem in advertising will be how to sell to values increasingly geared to processes, not things. Sales appeals directed toward the values of individualism, experimentalism, person-centeredness, direct experience, and some forms of pleasure and escape will need to tap intangibles — human relationships, feelings, dreams, and hopes — rather than tangible things or explicit actions.... Messages will need to convey genuine warmth, emotional content, and a sense of reality. ... [Messages should give] a sense of the cosmic, of healthiness, simplicity, ruggedness, openness, and the interconnectedness of things.[28]

Most kinds of cultural production, children's toys, for example, cannot be understood without examining the production of consumption.

For most people, toys are a given, a reality there to be purchased and given to children to delight them, with few persons ever reflecting on toys as a cultural vehicle. They know of course that children have toys and play with them. Children *love* toys, and in fact toys are good for children. After all, "play is the child's work." A minority of these persons might even be ready to admit that toys are a part of the child's culture, of the child's world of meaning, and that one can understand the child-culture of a past period by examining the now-antique toys produced for that time. However, in such an approach, these concepts, toys and culture, still remain inert. Acknowledging that the toys children play with help define the world of meaning (i.e., culture) they inhabit does not take one very far in understanding how the culture of toys actually works. One still might not be able, for instance, to think about the various ways toys are produced. The matter is important since the *processes of production* of toys get at the full complexity and reality of how they do, finally, help fashion a world of meaning of children. The importance of understanding this "fashioning" of a world of meaning for children is suggested by the following paraphrase of an editorial from the *New Yorker* (25 February 1985, pp. 26–27) entitled "Huggaland," a report written by Lillian Ross, on the gigantic toy fair held each year in New York City:

> I got an eyeful and earful at the Eighty-second Annual American International Toy Fair, where toys producers hawk their wares to representatives of marketing firms. This year, a young and effervescent sales/public relations representative told me Kenner Toys is out in front producing human-like "goodness toys." Being out in front means something special in an industry generating each year 12 billion dollars in retail sales. This year, she went on, your "plush" is definitely in, pushing your hi-tech to second place.
>
> For 1985 she chirped excitedly to me, Kenner's leading edge in "goodness toys" comes from the Hugga Bunch dolls — plushy, cute, and above all, huggable dolls — eight of 'em if your child wants the full collection. These cuties give children the impetus to show their loving feelings. Kenner believes in expressing warm feelings. And who could resist these eight creatures in their Hugga Nook, their home in Huggaland, all dressed in their cuddly huglies? With these Hugga

toys, each child gets a Hugga Bunch pledge: hug each Hugga toy at least once a day. Be a hugger.

Toys provide an instructive example of cultural production for those parents becoming aware that through toys, an agenda not their own is being passed on to their children. Actually, these latent agendas for children tend to bypass the full agency of most parents, who, on the issue of toys, tend to become passive spectators with the money to select toys but without the ability to contest them. Very few toys today are produced by parents for children. Those who orchestrate the play of children have as much power over them as those who tell them stories. One critic of cosmetic toys for quite young children claimed, "It is all about the sexualization of little girls."[29] Others object to the militarization of children through war toys. Costa Rica, a nation without an army, has passed a law outlawing war toys as a way of forestalling the militarization of its children.

However, as I have explained in previous paragraphs, the matter of toys cannot be adequately understood without probing their marketing or what I have called the production of their consumption. In the mass-production of toys, long before many companies have even entered the concrete production process, they have already begun producing their marketing strategies, such as televised cartoon series for children. A growing literature sheds light on this "production of consumption" as it affects children.[30]

"Those who orchestrate the play of children have as much power over them as those who tell them stories." If my claim here is true, then parents and others who care about children must question their own agency in the face of the TV stories their children have access to. With television sets on in the average home more than eight hours a day, the narratives children see there have an influence far more subtle and powerful than space permits me to explain here. Readers may want to explore some of the writing on this topic.[31] Parents who intently study books about child-rearing to give them information about how to shape a child's sleeping or eating habits may overlook entirely the child's televiewing habits. The issue here is about the agency appropriate to those professing to have at heart the deepest long-term interests of the child. A related issue involves helping children themselves think about the false promises being made to them in ads for toys. The HBO video mentioned earlier is a good example of how this can be done.

Parents are not the only ones who have the interests of children at heart and who are concerned with the influences on children in the time of electronic communications. Using the same cultural pollution metaphor as Gustavo Gutiérrez, Jacques D'Amboise, a dancer who has been teaching dance to inner-city children, put his concerns this way:

> ... [T]he single most terrible thing we are doing to our children, I believe, is polluting them. I don't mean just with smog and crack, but by not teaching them the civilizing things we have taken millions [sic] of years to develop. . . .
>
> I think of each person as a trunk that's up in the attic. What are you going to put in the trunk? Are you going to put in machine guns, loud noises, foul language, dirty books and ignorance? Because, if you do, that's what is going to be left after you, that's what your children are going to have, and will determine the world of the future. Or are you going to fill that trunk with music, dance, poetry, literature, good manners and loving friends?
>
> I say, fill your trunk with the best that is available to you from the wealth of human culture. Those things will nourish you and your children. You can clean up your own environment and pass it on to the next generation. That's why I teach dance.[32]

Such sensitivity is not for parents alone but for anyone concerned about the sort of life vision we present to others.

Someone might ask, Why can I not just enjoy what I read, see, or hear, without asking any questions except did I like it? I do not discount the value of the "Did I like it" question. If anything, critique enriches and hones the appreciation and "liking" of artifacts. Critique is part of the call to be human, the call to become a co-producer of the world of meaning and not merely a consumer. To be co-producers of their own world of meaning is the vocation of persons of all ages, children included. The studies of children's games by Iona and Peter Opie demonstrate the extent to which children have originated, controlled, and passed on orally their forms of play down through centuries and across national and language barriers.[33]

When judgment is eroded, life itself becomes diminished. People lose something crucial to human agency: their capacity to think. At every point in the production process there are human hands and human faces, but often hidden from view. The questions posed here invite those faces to take center stage to be seen and recognized for their important part in what has been produced. Only in such a process can the often unexamined matter of *human intention* be also brought into the critical spotlight.[34] These questions should have significance for religious persons. They are called to an active kind of judgment, using the yardstick of the religious understandings they claim are the ultimate ones.

## Full Participation in the Production of Religious Meaning: A Roman Catholic Example

If my claim is true that a human person is called to be a co-producer of the world of meaning and not merely a consumer, then it should also be true of the world of religious meaning. Yet the ways persons are excluded from the full production of religious meaning remain unclear to many. Perhaps examining the role of youth in the Christian churches could provide some clarifications of the issues.

In *Laborem Exercens,* his encyclical on labor, Pope John Paul II highlights the principle that all persons have not only a right to income but also a right to production, that is, to engage in processes of production. Income allows a per-

son to become a consumer, but the Pope insists that every
person has a natural right also to produce, not just consume. The right to a job is the right to exercise the human
vocation of producer. This principle has yet to be applied
to lay persons in local communities. As far as I can determine, the youth ministry efforts that in fact are influencing
young people toward discipleship do so because they allow
the young to become co-producers of the religious culture in
which they stand. And the efforts that are failing are those
that reduce young people to the status of consumers, accepting doctrinal capital on a "handout" basis and putting
it to good use. Such a process is quite different from laying open to them the community's resources and inviting
them to use them for engaging in the production of meaning:
through dialogue, through struggling with the problematic
situation of today's world, through allowing the questioning
of assumptions and claims, including doctrinal ones, found
among many young people, and especially through action
for justice.

Luke's Emmaus account (24:35) provides a portrait of this
sort of cultural production. Jesus enters the journey of his
disciples in the midst of their puzzlement, does not disrupt it
but, through his interest and questions, encourages them to
recount for him the matter they had been talking over. Jesus
builds on their struggle to understand and invites the disciples to become co-producers of religious understanding. He
does not start off with the know-it-all oration that reduces
his fellow travelers to passivity.

Participation in the life of the community of the church
means participation in the creation of the culture of the
church in the sense that one comes to an authentic, and very
possibly an original, word about the quest for discipleship in
our time.[35] The culture of the local church emerges from the
struggles of many individuals to express in words and deeds
their option for the Gospel and the outcome of that option.
But nobody participates in the creation of culture without
participation in the creation or re-forming of the polity of
that culture. To have a say in the production of the culture

of the local church means likewise having a say in the way its power is used.

The stumbling block to the full participation of the laity in the church comes when they are invited to participate in the *reproduction* of religious meaning but not in the true, original production of that meaning. In the Roman Catholic communion, this is a special stumbling block to women, who, because of gender, are deemed *permanently* lay, and to youth, who, because of age, are *exclusively* lay. Full participation in the life of the church becomes culturally authentic only to the extent that participants have the opportunity to speak to the policies that affect them, to struggle to name the values they will suffer for, to communicate to others those values, and to be confronted by the values lived by others. Nothing shuts off this process as fully as manifestos and proclamations handed down from on high.

Pope John Paul II, despite his call for full participation in economic production and his ringing critique of some forms of cultural production, and despite his call to the young to join in cultural critique and resistance, seems insensitive to the issue of religious production within Roman Catholicism. He does not extend to the laity a role in cultural production as I have explained it here. His apostolic exhortation, *Christifideles Laici,* is filled with inspiring passages about lay participation in the church and its mission, all of which seem to invite full participation in the production of meaning — until one gets to Section 22 and the following paragraphs:

> In a primary position in the Church are the *ordained ministries,* that is, the ministries *that come from the Sacrament of Orders.* [Here and below all emphases are in the original.] In fact, with the mandate to make disciples of all nations, the Lord Jesus chose and constituted the apostles — seed of the People of the New Covenant and origin of the Hierarchy — to form and to rule the priestly people. The mission of the apostles, which the Lord Jesus continues to entrust to the

Pastors of his people, is a true service, significantly referred to in Sacred Scripture as *"diakonia,"* namely,
service or ministry. The ministries receive the charism of
the Holy Spirit from the Risen Christ, in uninterrupted
succession from the apostles, through the Sacrament
of Orders: from him they receive the authority and
sacred power to serve the Church, acting *in persona
Christi Capitis* (in the person of Christ, the Head) and
to gather her in the Holy Spirit through the Gospel and
the Sacraments.

The ordained ministries, apart from the persons who
receive them, are a grace for the entire Church. These
ministries express and realize a participation in the
priesthood of Jesus Christ that is different, not simply in
degree but in essence, from the participation given to all
the lay faithful through Baptism and Confirmation. On
the other hand, the ministerial priesthood ... essentially
has the royal priesthood of all the faithful as it aim and
is ordered to it.[36]

In a process of giving with the right hand and taking back
with the left, these paragraphs offer differences in participation, "not only in degree but in essence." Such terminology
and the cast of mind it reflects undercut participation in
cultural production, as becomes more clear in following
sections:

... A more ordered and fruitful ecclesial practice of the
ministries entrusted to the lay faithful can be achieved
if all the particular Churches faithfully respect ... the
essential difference between the ministerial priesthood
and the common priesthood, and the difference between
the ministries derived from the Sacrament of Orders
and those derived from the Sacraments of Baptism and
Confirmation. [Sec. 23]

[Among the criteria for evaluating the ecclesiality
of lay groups are] *the responsibility of professing the
Catholic faith,* embracing and proclaiming the truth
about Christ, the Church and humanity, in obedience

to the Church's Magisterium, as the Church [presumably meaning, the Magisterium] interprets it...; *the witness to a strong and authentic communion* in filial relationship to the Pope, in total adherence to the belief that he is the perpetual and visible center of unity of the universal Church, and with the local bishop.... The communion with Pope and Bishop must be expressed in loyal readiness to embrace the doctrinal teachings and pastoral initiatives of both Pope and Bishop. [Sec. 30]

In these passages I find an incomplete understanding of cultural agency and the dangers that flow from such misunderstanding. Almost in contradiction to other glowing passages about lay participation, these suggest that, in the end, lay persons have quite limited forms of participation in the church. Overlooking the differences between cultural production and cultural reproduction, the passages imply that the true agency remains in the hands of an elite, who, of their very nature, cannot be contested.[37]

At the beginning of this chapter I stated that I sought to name and highlight cultural production because it involves procedures open to our analysis. I also claimed that understanding cultural production and how it works leads us to a much more specific and "operative" concept of culture than the vague, inert one I claim so many people have. Here, at the end, I have examined cultural production in the church itself, as envisaged in a single document, and found that John Paul II's insightful critique of the electronic communication of meaning is not matched by a similar critique of the church's own processes of the production of meaning. One could fruitfully examine a series of church documents about the communication of the Gospel from the perspective of cultural production.

Readers may now see that I have in mind two moments important to cultural analysis: one of contestation, the other of accommodation. Each is the fruit of judgment. Contestation is the stance of opposition and distancing taken when some cultural product fails to meet religious/

humanistic criteria. Religion itself and its products must fall
under such judgment. Accommodation is the stance of ap-
proval and welcome for cultural products that meet norms
of humanization. Of course, not every aspect of culture,
some quite complex, is open to such clear categories of ap-
proval or disapproval. Certain features may be welcomed,
while others rejected, making summary judgments difficult,
if not impossible. The exercise of religious authority, specifically, the example of papal authority cited here, might be,
under religious/humanistic scrutiny, judged an example of
yes-and-no ambiguity.

## Questions to Foster Cultural Analysis

1. Who is producing this material and in whose interests?
   If a single person, does s/he function as a mouthpiece
   for some group remaining in the background? Does the
   person represent in any way the interests and/or point
   of view of any particular group?

2. Who controls, in two senses, the medium for which this
   material is being produced? First, who makes the editorial decisions? Who hires the writer(s)? Second, who
   controls the medium economically? How does this economic control affect decisions about the signification
   actually being produced here?

   Notice how asking this last question in a particular
   way lets us peek beneath the surface of the medium
   itself to see who else may be there exercising power.

3. What is the history of this medium? What have been the
   significant shifts in it? What changes are going on now
   and how do they function?

4. How does the medium actually function? What complex interests are at work here? In the instance of magazines and newspapers, how is the print medium tied
   to the structures of marketing and advertising? Is the

printed news expected to attract advertising revenue? Do those who pay the costs of advertising influence the editorial direction?

NB: Such questions can be asked about the functioning of any medium.

5. What judgments can be made of the value or lack of it in these procedures or their final product?

## NOTES

1. "Mass Culture and Critical Pedagogy," chapter 3 of Stanley Aronowitz and Henry Giroux, *Education under Siege* (Granby, Mass.: Bergin and Garvey, 1985), pp. 47–55, at 51. Chapter 3 may have been written entirely by Aronowitz.

2. A 1989 study of network TV, co-sponsored by the National Commission on Working Women, found that 15 percent of producers, 25 percent of writers, and 9 percent of directors were women. See Andrea Adelson, "Study Attacks Women's Roles in TV," *New York Times*, 19 November 1990, p. C18.

3. Karl Marx and Friedrich Engels, *The German Ideology* (*GI*), as cited in Raymond Williams, "Ideology," chapter 4 of *Marxism and Literature* (New York: Oxford University Press, 1977), p. 58.

4. *Marxism and Literature*, p. 59. Though *GI* is under joint authorship of Engels and Marx, I will refer to the ideas as Marx's, in keeping with my (and Williams's) references to later "Marxist" theory.

5. Other passages from *GI* indicate that Marx's intention was to show not the separation between the material social processes of life and consciousness, but the close connection between them:

> The ruling ideas are nothing more than the ideal expression of the dominant material relationships, the dominant material relationships grasped as ideas. (GI, 39)

> Consciousness can never be anything else than conscious existence, and the existence of men in their actual life-process. If in all *ideology* [emphasis added] men [*sic*] and their circumstances appear upside down as in a *camera obscura*, this phenomenon arises just as much from their historical life-process as the inversion of objects on the retina does from their physical life-process. (GI, 14)

6. *Marxism and Literature*, p. 59.

7. Ibid., pp. 61–62.

8. Ibid., p. 70. Williams makes this same point at greater length in an earlier section of *Marxism and Literature*.

Signification, the social creation of meanings through the use of formal signs, is then a practical material activity; it is indeed, literally, a means of production. It is a specific form of that practical consciousness [i.e., consciousness being acted out] which is inseparable from all social material activity. It is not, as formalism would make it, and as the idealist theory of expression had from the beginning assumed, an operation of and within "consciousness," which then becomes a state or a process separated, a priori, from social material activity. It is, on the contrary, at once a distinctive material process — the making of signs — and, in the central quality of its distinctiveness as practical consciousness, is involved from the beginning in all other human social and material activity. (p. 38)

9. Ibid., p. 19.

10. Ibid., p. 37.

11. New York: Oxford University Press, 1984.

12. Two other writers whose analyses of language as cultural signification have had special value for me are: George Steiner, *Language and Silence* (New York: Atheneum Books, 1967), and Czeslaw Milosz, *The Witness of Poetry* (Cambridge, Mass.: Harvard University Press, 1983), especially the last chapter, "Ruins and Poetry."

13. Raymond Williams, *Television, Technology and Cultural Form* (New York: Schocken Books, 1975), pp. 11–12.

14. Williams distinguishes between a technical invention and a technology. A technical invention is the development of a particular skill or a device that applies that skill. A technology is a body of knowledge appropriate to the development of a technical skill *and* the conditions for the practical use and application of a range of devices applying that skill. See Raymond Williams, ed., *Contact: Human Communication and Its History* (London: Thames and Hudson, 1981), pp. 226–27; also, Raymond Williams, *The Sociology of Culture* (New York: Schocken Books, 1982), pp. 108–9.

15. An example of such analysis that opens avenues for further study is Raymond Williams, "Means of Communication as Means of Production," in *Problems in Materialism and Culture* (London: Verso, 1980), pp. 50–63.

16. Thomas Whiteside's lengthy examination of the choices open in developing home cable television ("Onward and Upward with the Arts: Cable — I, II, III," *New Yorker* [20, 27 May, 3 June 1985]) deserves careful study for verbatim promises made by media executives that were, in the long run, not kept.

Also important are the writings of Everett C. Parker about the Federal Communications Act of 1934, which set up the Federal Communications Commission with a specific mandate, gradually (and illegally) eroded since then. See, for instance, William B. Kennedy and Everett C. Parker,

"On Control: A Discussion of the Ethical and Moral Issues Arising from Current Communication Policies and Practices," *Religious Education* 82, no. 2 (1987): 203–17.

17. Ben H. Bagdikian, "The Lords of the Global Village," *The Nation* (12 June 1989): 807. On this same point of social control, see Mark Crispin Miller, "The Hipness unto Death," in *Boxed-In: The Culture of TV* (Evanston, Ill.: Northwestern University Press, 1988), p. 11.

18. Some examples of writing on these questions are: Robert A. White, "Mass Communication and Culture: Transition to a New Paradigm," *Journal of Communication* 33, no. 3 (1983): 279–301; Hamid Mowlana, "Mass Media and Culture: Toward an Integrated Theory," in *Intercultural Communication Theory: Current Perspectives,* edited by William B. Gudykunst (Beverly Hills, Calif.: Sage Publications, 1983). Of special importance is the two-volume edited work of Armand Mattelart and Seth Siegelaub, *Communication and Class Struggle* (New York: International General, 1979).

19. See Stuart Ewen, *All-Consuming Images: The Politics of Style in Contemporary Culture* (New York: Basic Books, 1988).

20. Bill Fore, former communications specialist at the National Council of Churches in New York, offered a particularly sharp example of critical demystification about the news coverage of the Persian Gulf War in 1991. He analyzed the televised versions of what happened by viewing them through three lenses: (1) television as signifier, (2) television as economics, and (3) television as gratifier-entertainer. His analysis of the production of news is worth study. See William F. Fore, "Analyzing the Military-News Complex," *The Christian Century* (17 April 1991): 422–23.

21. Williams, "Means of Communication," p. 60.

22. Ibid., pp. 60–62, passim.

23. New York Area Educators for Social Responsibility, *Action News* 60 (15 May 1991).

24. See for example the questions raised in Carlin Romano, "The Grisly Truth about Bare Facts," in R. K. Manoff and Michael Schudson, eds., *Reading the News* (New York: Pantheon Books, 1987), pp. 38–78.

25. This is the same kind of thinking I applaud in William F. Fore's analysis of news coverage of the Persian Gulf War (note 20 above).

26. I do not minimize the legal complexities of this matter. A seminal essay about the shift in the production of art is: Walter Benjamin, "The Work of Art in the Age of Mechanical Reproduction," in Hannah Arendt, ed., *Illuminations* (New York: Harcourt, Brace, 1968), pp. 219–53. The writings of Catharine A. MacKinnon provide helpful perspectives on the arguments of some feminists in this matter of censorship. See her bibliography in "Desire and Power: A Feminist Perspective," in Cary Nelson and Lawrence Grossberg, eds., *Marxism and the Interpretation of Culture* (Chicago: University of Chicago Press, 1988), pp. 105–21.

27. See Williams's fine essay on the history of the advertising in Britain, "Advertising: The Magic System," in *Problems in Materialism and Culture,* pp. 170–95. More recently (1988), Stuart Ewen's fine, detailed *All-Consuming Images.*

28. Cited in James Atlas, "Beyond Demographics," *Atlantic Monthly* (October 1984): 49–58.

29. Anne-Marie Schiro, "Play-Cosmetics for Children: Dissenting Voices Are Heard," *New York Times* (21 February 1981), p. 13.

30. Some useful titles: Fred M. Hechinger, "About Education: TV's Pitch to Children," *New York Times* (17 March 1987), p. C9; Philip H. Dougherty, "Advertising: Inside Children's Television," *New York Times* (20 May 1987), p. D19; Glenn Collins, "Controversy about Toys, TV Violence," *New York Times* (12 December 1985), p. C1; Richard W. Stevenson, "The Selling of Toy 'Concepts,'" *New York Times* (14 December 1985), p. 33; Peter J. Boyer, "Toy-Based TV: Effects on Children Debated," *New York Times* (3 February 1986), p. A1ff.; Craig Simpson, "The Violence of War Toys," *The Non-Violent Activist* (November–December 1985), pp. 3–6; Nancy Carlsson-Paige and Diane E. Levin, *Who's Calling the Shots? How to Respond Effectively to Children's Fascination with War Play and War Toys* (Philadelphia: New Society Publishers, 1990); Rita Reif, "Antiques: Toys That Go Beyond," *New York Times* (2 March 1986), p. H26; "Huggaland: Report on 82nd Annual International Toy Fair," *New Yorker* (25 February 1985), pp. 26–27. See also the annual report on children's toys published the second week of each December in the *New Yorker.*

I call special attention to the Carlsson-Paige/Levin book above for its history of war toys, highlighting recent shifts. Toys that militarize children call for detailed analysis.

31. Among titles I would recommend are: Robert M. Liebert and Joyce Sprafkin, *The Early Window: Effects of Television on Children and Youth* (New York: Pergamon Press, 1988); William B. Kennedy, "Understanding Media: An Interview with Robert Liebert," *Religious Education* 82, no. 2 (1987): 191–202; Marie Winn, *The Plug-in Drug: Television, Children, and the Family* (New York: Bantam Books, 1978), and *Unplugging the Plug-in Drug* (New York: Viking-Penguin, 1987); Frances Moore Lappe, *What to Do after You Turn Off the TV* (New York: Ballantine, 1985). For me, the most provocative work on the problems caused by TV is Postman's *Amusing Ourselves to Death: Public Discourse in the Age of Show Business* (New York: Viking Penguin, 1985). Also of special value is Miller, "The Hipness unto Death."

32. Jacques D'Amboise, "I Show a Child What Is Possible," *Boston Sunday Globe Parade,* 6 August 1989, p. 6.

33. Iona and Peter Opie, *Children's Games in Street and Playground* (New York: Oxford University Press, 1969), and *The Singing Game* (New

York: Oxford University Press, 1985). These books provide important reading for anyone interested in forms of cultural agency. They could be well compared with certain of the hymns cited in Susan S. Tamke, *Make a Joyful Noise unto the Lord: Hymns as a Reflection of Victorian Social Attitudes* (Athens: Ohio University Press, 1978). See especially chapter 4: "Hymns for Children," a study of Victorian hymns created by adults as a way of controlling the behavior of children through moralizing.

34. In *Television,* pp. 119–22, Williams astutely notes how easily concrete human intentions can be lost to sight in a blizzard of abstract social terminology.

35. My own interest in this question was sparked by Boff's claim that "the organizing axis of a society is its specific mode of production," a conviction he then applies to the church. In my own translation of Boff's ideas, the "faithful" occupy a social position in keeping with their lower-class status. They tend to have the Gospel allotted to them on a kind of hand-out basis by the ruling class, the ecclesiastical bosses, hard at work to consolidate their power. In the early church, however, there was a different mode of production, more symmetric and participatory. See Leonardo Boff, "Theological Characteristics of a Grassroots Church," in S. Torres and J. Eagleson, eds., *The Challenge of Basic Christian Communities* (Maryknoll, N.Y.: Orbis, 1981).

36. *Christifideles Laici: On the Vocation and the Mission of the Lay Faithful in the Church and in the World* (Vatican City: Libreria Editrice Vaticana, 1988), no. 22, pp. 56–57. All emphases are as in the original.

37. In 1989, the Vatican Congregation for the Doctrine of the Faith made clear that professors of theology and a range of other "teachers" were also to be consumers of religious understanding or, at most, conduits for the production of officialdom. The Congregation proposed an oath of faith and fealty be taken by such teachers. See "Doctrinal Congregation Publishes Faith Profession and Oath," *Origins* 18, no. 40 (16 March 1989): 661, 663.

*Chapter 5*

# A THEORY OF IMAGES IN CULTURAL SYSTEMS

A conviction behind this book is that we now live in an "image culture." With film, television, and print technology allowing for the cheap reproduction of graphics in multi-colors, almost all in the post-industrial West are immersed in images. Society is so much awash in them that the prevalence of images is a dominant characteristic of our time. Some educators now find that students are less and less able to analyze an argument in logical categories. Instead, they state the argument's thesis and then seek to find a graphic illustration to either support it or rebut it.[1] In the "time of the sign," it becomes more and more natural for young people — and most others — to think via images, examples, and narratives. When asked to deal with ideas or analyze a written argument, they are likely to offer instead a personal conviction or preference which they then back up with a narrative.

One might expect the proliferation of images to foster an enhanced imagination as a characteristic of contemporary sensibility. In my view this proliferation has fostered the opposite, a diminished imagination. Though steeped in images, most persons in our society do not seem to be able to think about images. They have little idea of how images function in shaping their consciousness. When some reality influences us at the same that we do not have a language with which to be aware of it, the influence is increased. The images cramming the consciousness of many today tend to be pre-set, borrowed images used in non-imaginative, literal ways to name and interpret life. These are the images handed on to them via film and TV.

Many seem to be like the young man in Peter Shaffer's play *Equus,* who, in his madness, can only express himself in the jingles of TV commercials.[2] Shaffer implies that naming reality via the pre-set, stereotyped clichés of advertising is the shape of madness in our time. So ironically, we live in an image culture with people immersed in images and using them to illustrate their own convictions, but at the same time impaired in their creative imaginal development.

My purpose here is to provide an understanding of images that will assist us in cultural analysis. As a signifying system by which a social order is communicated and experienced, culture cannot be adequately understood in its specific functioning without an awareness of images and how they function. In the time of electronic communication, cultural agency involves being able to think about images, to question them, and if necessary, to find alternative ones. I wish to examine two kinds of images, each kind with its own subsets: iconic or representational images and metaphoric-perceptual images.

## Iconic Images

Iconic images are what we usually mean when we use the word "image." These images are representational in the sense that they depict some person, place, object, event, or narrative.[3] These images are pictures we see with our eyes rather than with our "mind's eye," the imagination. Iconic images, so common in current society, can be understood through the following scheme classifying them according to function: (1) Graphic representations in a single frame; (2) graphic representations in sequential, internally coherent frames, i.e., frames linked to form a narrative; and (3) graphic representations in sequential, internally incoherent, externally coherent frames.

The first kind of image, a representation in a single frame, is a picture that is complete in itself. Such a picture is not run in sequence with other pictures, and does not take its significance from its place in a sequence the way a single "frame" of a film does. However, many representations in single frames, though not needing other frames to complement them, cannot be fully understood without their connection to matters outside the picture's frame, or some wider context. For example, a picture in a newspaper might have little meaning until it is connected to a news story for which it serves as an illustration. A picture in an art gallery is connected to a painter, a period, a body of other work. In addition, its gallery context lends it a significance it might not have leaning against a cellar wall. Similarly, many graphic advertisements in print are single-frame representations, but their significance is found in the commercial text accompanying the picture. Most print images are of this kind.

Many people never think about the prevalence of these images. They surround us so constantly that we tend to take them for granted. In fact, such images form a kind of visual horizon in our everyday life. We see them on billboards, in magazines, in newspapers, on windows, on the interior (and exterior) of buses and trains. To get a sense of the difference these single-frame images make in our environment we would have to compare their current use to their near absence in newspapers and magazines published before print technology allowed for pictures to be beamed electronically to newspaper offices and graphically reproduced in high resolution, and later, in color. Such publications had few pictures compared with current ones. One could even devise a numerical measurement of the amount of printed text to pictorial text per page as compared with similar publications today. For centuries, societies have produced graphic means of advertising goods and services, either in such symbols as the triple spheres logo for a pawnshop or the picture of a horse for a stable or in simple lettered signs. What has changed is not the fact but the volume and vividness of such representations today.[4]

Iconic images of the second type are graphic representations in sequential, internally coherent frames. These are the images in sequence that come to form a film or a television presentation. Such images work to form some kind of narrative that has its own coherence. Many kinds of visual "narratives" fit into this category, even though they may not bear much resemblance to a full-length film or a television drama or even seem to have much narrative structure at all in the usual sense. A television ad, for example, is a shortened narrative, a "slice of life" scenario, often with an abrupt beginning and an even more abrupt ending. The narrative may start in the middle of some action and then simply stop, with a voice explaining the significance of the brief scenario. Among these sequential images I include television news and what are called "game shows" and "talk shows" because of these traces of a loose narrative structure of beginning, middle, and end.

Visual images in coherent sequences are not new. They can be found in medieval tapestries, in frescoes and metal work, and in stained glass windows. What is new is their proliferation and accessibility, which began in this century and increased dramatically within the past forty-five years or so. Today, most persons in the West are as immersed in such sequential narratives as they are in single-frame representations. As already noted, current estimates are that, in the average home, the television is on eight-and-a-half hours every day. Recent analyses show that the only activity a child in the U.S. engages in that takes up more time than television is sleeping: between the ages of six and eighteen the average U.S. child spends about 16,000 hours in front of a TV set.[5]

The fact that television became a reality in U.S. homes only after 1945 suggests that this single development has changed dramatically the life structure — what people actually do with their time — of most people. Once people came to have access within their own homes to graphic representations in sequentially coherent frames (representations previously available only in movie theaters), they could, theoretically at least, watch them without limitations. Considering the way stories shape our world of signification, easy access to filmed images represented a huge cultural shift, but *unlimited* access to filmed and televised narratives was a cultural shift so great that its full significance may be beyond assessment. The various shifts in the style and technique of the actual sequences of this imagery call for detailed treatment not possible here.[6]

Iconic images of the third type involve graphic representations in sequential, internally incoherent, but externally coherent frames. These images are the most recently developed. A prime example would be those so-called music videos which use non-associated sequences of images that do not form a narrative. Coherence comes from outside the images, say, in the music which provides an external bond or in the voice and possible appearance of a singer in several frames. In this case — which is not true even of all "music videos" — coherence is imposed subjectively by the viewer from outside the images. To a certain extent, poetry is similar, requiring the reader to work at making connections. Externally imposed coherence is also a characteristic of many slide shows, where music provides an editorial comment on a series of images only loosely tied together around some theme, such as "youth in the world" or some social issue. Though a narrative, properly so-called, has its own plot line with sequences of action and lines of agency,[7] these images cannot be logically plotted but have a sequence that simply is the way it is. One might even say that many sequences in music, say of a particular composer or musical period, are more "logical" in the sense of being predictable, than are some of these image sequences. At least the musical sequence can be predicted by understanding the musical logic of a particular composer. To embrace or even cope with internally incoherent sequential images, one must allow oneself to move beyond logical sequence.

My neat distinction here between internally coherent and externally coherent visual sequences becomes, on closer examination, more complex. An examination of some of the second type of iconic images, both in film and TV, shows how they can take on characteristics of the third type. Thus a particular narrative can have sequences of events that, when examined closely, have little or no coherence. Persons may appear, and they may perform an action crucial for moving the action forward, but the viewer has little understanding of where they came from or why they happened to be in a particular place at a particular time or even why they did what they did. It is possible, then, to have a narrative that purports to offer an intelligible sequence of events but in fact does not possess one. What seems to happen in such narratives is that incoherence is being substituted for coherence *and is not expected to make any difference.* This sort of narrative is very different from a play by Beckett, for example, which depicts incoherence as a critique of modern life; instead these other narratives seem to say that agency and coherence are not significant. The long-term effects on consciousness of such narratives remain to be seen, but Neil Postman, writing about TV in general, proposes the following thesis that could be applied to the incoherence I have just described:

> Make no mistakes about it: the TV curriculum embodies a clear and powerful philosophy concerning the nature of reality. Its axioms include that history is bunk, that hierarchies are arbitrary, that problems have no antecedents, that the future is not worth dwelling upon, that randomness is uncontrollable. I believe the word is Dadaism. In psychiatric circles, it is known as chronic depression.[8]

Many people in a visual culture are conditioned for accepting incoherence by the constant interruption of otherwise coherent narratives with commercials in an entirely different emotional key. When such interruptions cease to jar viewers, incoherence has come to be normalized. Readers should note that at this point, except for the Postman passage, I have tried to be descriptive instead of normative or evaluative. I am aware that the way television narratives work is quite complex, having complex effects, many of them beneficial.

In a fine work on television drama, Helena Sheehan warns us not to deal with television is a reductionistic way:

> The paradoxical power of television is such that it is, and does, virtually all that is said of it. Its complexity is such that both claims and counter-claims capture something of the multi-faceted truth of it. The best and worst opinions of it generally have their justification.[9]

However, if something has, in fact, shifted in many persons' tolerance for incoherence, those concerned about consciousness need to be aware of it and ponder its implications. At issue here is our own ability to think and evaluate the influences impinging on our own lives.

## Iconic Images and Mimesis

Crucial for understanding the significance of iconic images is recognizing their power to move those who see them toward mimesis or imitation. The tendency toward mimesis is a seminal feature of human nature that has, up till now, received too little attention, especially considering its power in directing human behavior. In her comment that "it is axiomatic of a society that we are who [sic] we celebrate," Barbara Goldsmith has touched on the social implications of mimesis in our time:[10]

> But the need to celebrate other human beings — some symbolic, some real — is a continuing psychic and societal fact. Throughout history, the accomplishments of these individuals have provided a pattern for our aspirations; their frailties have bolstered our self-images. Celebrity worship, the psychoanalyst Ernest van den Haag says, is directly traceable to the basic and continuing need for authority figures, the first of whom are our parents.[11]

Goldsmith, to whose ideas I will return in a later chapter, observes that though our deep-seated need to have individuals to celebrate has remained relatively stable, our society has not. As a result of many developments, electronic communications but one of them, we have now come to create synthetic celebrities, famed for their images, not their deeds. Among their number are those who have become "celebrities" because we have seen them perform in various electronic narratives.

However, even on a more individual level, a human being is a mimetic creature. Humans tend to imitate behavior they see in others, a fact filled with as many positive possibilities as negative ones. Most persons recognize the tendency in children where it functions in a bald, undisguised way. Children, especially very young children, are the quintessential mimics. Parents report embarrassment when they behold a young child imitating parental behavior that the parents themselves dislike. On the positive side, children can and do imitate the good behavior they find in others. Religious groups have been founded partly on this realization. Children acquire their first desire for skills such as reading and writing or for the patterned behavioral skills we call virtues by observing others; part of the acquisition of any skill involves imitation. What is true of children is in fact true of all persons, at least as a tendency.

Even when we look at a single-frame representation, a photo of some person or a place, we tend to mentally establish connections between what we see and what we already know. This person looks like X or this place is not so different from Y. If the person is of the same sex or race or age or social status as ours, then we tend to make a connection between ourselves and the person. We do not say, "This person is me," but rather something like, "This person is like me," or "I am like, or *could be* like, this person." What I am trying to get at here is the latent power of icons to trigger a way of imagining ourselves. In fact, for many centuries, religious imagery has been used in this way of inviting the viewer to imitate the qualities of the person or reality represented by the icon.[12] If imaginal power inhabits single-frame representations which are relatively inert when compared to the "live" images found in sequential, coherent frames, then the moving images of film and television have an exponentially greater mimetic power, some of it enhancing the quest for a deeper humanity.

There are also examples of the negative functioning of the imaginal, mimetic properties of iconic images. One is the evidence showing that the rise of violence in the U.S. coincides with the rise in the depiction of violence in film and television; or that the rise of sexual activity among early adolescents coincides with the increase of similar depictions on theater or home screens. So far none of this evidence claims to establish clear causative links between the depiction and the acts. Still for many, the circumstantial links are convincing, and certain studies provide evidence of connections difficult to dismiss.

A compelling, though disputed, analysis of violent, dominative iconic images has been set forth by feminist lawyer Catharine MacKinnon. MacKinnon's concerns are about the dangers of representing reality in images that actually demean. Alarmed by the sexual brutalization and exploitation of women by means of pornography, she claims that such representations do not simply *represent* reality; they also "construct reality." Though ways of seeing tend to be overlooked, MacKinnon stares intently at the images and their consequences.

A fundamental point in MacKinnon's analysis is a persistent examination of the connection in our society between power and the production of images. "[P]ower constructs the appearance of reality by silencing the voices of the powerless, by excluding them from access to authoritative discourse."[13] Images are produced that depict women, not just as less than men but as being brutalized or sexually assaulted. Such images are defended by many as the expression of free speech, even though in the process they erode the actual freedoms of women to be persons in the world. In the name of freedom of speech, women are thus denied equal protection under the law, which allows them to be imagined graphically as objects of exploitation.

Some find these to be extravagant claims, and to be sure, they have generated intense controversy. I find MacKinnon's passionate eloquence about the evils of dehumanizing representations compelling and her overall argument convincing, though difficult issues like censorship are not easily resolved. The cogency of her claims becomes clearer if one accepts her fundamental conviction: Images construct reality; they define how things are. Pornography defines a woman in pornographic terms: as unequal; as a plaything for men; as one whose domination and exploitation are legally found to be neutral. This ultimately gives permission to men to treat women according to this definition. The condition of the way women are imaged becomes the condition of the way women are treated. Though not unrelated to issues found in a vast literature on images, these claims about the power of images are new and probing.

When so many objections to pornography are limited to its erotic content, MacKinnon's critique is in terms of domination and the way images create a world of domination. This point must be clear for an accurate understanding of the following assessment of pornography:

> In pornography, there...is, in one place, all of the abuses that women had to struggle so long even to begin to articulate, all the *unspeakable* abuse: the rape, the battery, the sexual harassment, the prostitution, and the sexual abuse of children. Only in the pornography it is called something else: sex, sex, sex, sex, and sex, respectively. Pornography sexualizes rape, battery, sexual harassment, prostitution, and child sexual abuse; it thereby *celebrates, promotes, authorizes, and legitimizes them.* [Emphasis added.] More generally, it eroticizes the dominance and submission that is the dynamic common to them all. It makes hierarchy sexy and calls that "the truth about sex" or just a mirror reality. Through this process, pornography *constructs what a woman is as what men want from sex.* [Emphasis added.] This is what pornography means.[14]

To fully understand MacKinnon's position, a reader would do well to mentally add the word "the images of" before each mention of pornography, though she is referring also to an industry. These images are what celebrate, promote, authorize, and legitimize these de-humanizations of women and children. MacKinnon is sketching the human process by which a world of meaning is constructed that is counter-human.

In the case of pornography, clusters of images become "a constitutive practice" of a theory of gender inequality:

> [P]ornography is neither harmless fantasy nor a corrupt and confused misrepresentation of an otherwise natural sexual situation. It institutionalizes sexuality of male supremacy, fusing the eroticization of dominance and submission with the social construction of male and female. To the extent that gender is sexual, *pornography is part of constituting the meaning of that sexuality. Men treat women as who they see women as being.* [Emphasis added.] Pornography is that way.[15]

Applying these words to the question of imagery in general, we might say that what we see tends to construct a way of seeing and can, even further, become institutionalized in patterns of interaction between persons. Patterns of images can code our way of seeing. Would that those with explicit religious commitments understood the significance of this single point. Further, would that pastoral leaders could see its significance for themselves and the people in their congregations.

Images can, and indeed tend to, create assumptions about how the world really is. The verbs chosen by MacKinnon and found in my own comments get at the dynamism of images: "institutionalizes," "fusing," "constituting," "constructing," "coding," "creating." MacKinnon herself puts this dynamism forcefully when she notes that "pornography...is a political practice,"[16] to which I add, all depictions are a political practice, an exercise of power.[17] Though earlier than MacKinnon's writing, the Eron-Huesmann study of children and

TV violence showed that the 25 percent of nine-year-olds watching the most TV violence in 1960 were actually convicted of criminal offenses 150 percent more often in the following twenty-two years. Even here one cannot say that all 150 percent was due to violent entertainment. However, after taking into account ("controlling for") as many other factors as possible, the study concluded that a diet of TV violence was still the best predictor of convictions for juvenile crime ten years into the study and that there was a cause-effect relationship. There remains another possibility, that the study underestimated the relationship... since the study didn't begin until the children were nine years old. The impact of the roughly 4,500 hours of violent entertainment per child viewed before the beginning of the study was not measured. Another example of the mimetic character of iconic imagery is the Columbia University suicide study which showed roughly 20 additional suicides nationwide for each of four prime time suicide films on 1984–85 TV.[18]

Other examples of mimesis working through moving images are more subtle but convincing in the light of the above. In 1985, the *New York Times* reported the rise in citizens' complaints about police brutality, which had jumped in a single year by 600, to a high of 6,698 in 1984. The report sought to explain which factors may have contributed to this increase of complaints against police officers for purported mistreatment and excessive force. Among the explanations offered, the one given by a former commander of detectives in Chicago centered on the mimetic power of images. His assessment was that the movie and television glorification of violent police officers has encouraged many officers to use excessive force. "A lot of new and perhaps older cops are getting a confused message about their roles from what they see on TV and movie screens. The hero cop is no longer a straight arrow who does everything by the book. Now the media has cops, like Dirty Harry and Starsky and Hutch, who break the rules all the time."[19] Clearly an opinion, the suggestion of this former official offers one more indicator or clue that film and television images may not just depict reality but actually create it. They imagine for us how things are and how we could or should be.

In the absence of scientifically provable causal links, the film and television industries discount the claims of these studies. Such a denial is ironic in the face of the fact that TV advertising pays millions of dollars for thirty- or sixty-second spots on prime time. Are these expenditures made out of a conviction that TV does not influence viewers? Could executives justify such sums if they considered TV's influence so tenuous and dismissible that it is basically ineffective? Apparently these large sums spent to capture people's attention for such brief periods of time are considered well-spent because such ads do affect people's behavior. If advertising images affect behavior, perhaps the other images of film and television do also. U.S. playwright Steve Tesich warns us that he hasn't "seen a single anti-rape movie that doesn't promote rape. The very manner in which sexual scenes are shot causes rape to look like an activity that is energizing."[20] Still, media executives accused of influencing behavior through the violence or sexism they help produce deny that influence.

A final example of the suggestive mimetic power of sequential images comes from the film industry. Film critic Janet Maslin notes in passing in a film review the growing practice of placing brand-name products as foreground or background props in films. Product marketers pay to have their labels displayed even briefly as part of a film set. This is how her review ends:

> "Over the Top," which is one of Mr. Stallone's more muddled efforts but by no means a flop on the order of "F.I.S.T." or "RHINESTONE," includes a phenomenal number of plugs for various products. Brut cologne, Adidas sportswear and the Las Vegas Hilton are featured prominently and often. There are smaller but unmistakable plugs for Pepsi-Cola, Duracell batteries and many others.[21]

In this film, these products are displayed in the hand of an actor or on a billboard in the background or on a table in the

foreground — a matter that is never an accident and something for which companies producing these items pay the
film maker undisclosed sums. The practice illustrates a now-
accepted fact: that in subtle, latent ways the visual image
influences us.[22] Depictions that influence human behavior are
culturally significant.[23]

## The Significance of Iconic Images

Persons adept at questioning points of view and logical arguments in daily life may find that, *as viewers of images,* they
have not even considered the possibility of contesting representational images. In an image culture there is a tendency
for iconic images to be taken for granted, i.e., to be seen
but not examined. The examination of images, understanding how they function, and discerning in whose interests they
are produced, are all skills that can be learned.

Someone who helps us understand the *significance* of
iconic images is Margaret Miles, a theologian specializing in
non-discursive religious expression. To those seeking a better understanding of how these images function, Miles makes
available her rich understanding of the place of iconic images
in culture. She offers, for example, a helpful comparison between the medieval person's experience of religious images
and the modern person's involvement with media imagery.
Though Miles finds more differences than similarities, an
important similarity she notes is that in both cultures the
images are dealt with daily as a part of ordinary life. Not
encountered in museums, the images are "lived." Miles finds
three key differences between medieval and modern images.
The first of these is "the tremendous increase in the quantity
of images seen by a typical modern person."[24] Before the sixteenth century most people in the course of their lives would
have seen few images, many of them in their local church.
In contrast, persons today struggle with a kind of visual and
verbal overload. Their senses, in particular their vision, react
to this overload by tending to control and reduce data. In

Miles's view, "It is likely that our capacity for vision is — or will shortly be — congenitally fatigued by the sheer volume of images with which modern people cope."[25]

Miles's second difference between the medieval and the modern experience of iconic images is in the very understanding of physical vision in each period. The medieval understanding continued to be influenced by Augustine. Augustine theorized that vision itself is a fire that animates and warms the body, a fire that has special intensity behind the eyes. Vision is a ray projected to focus on the object and forming thereby a two-way channel allowing the viewer's energy and attention to touch the object and, in turn, allowing the object to return through the eye to be bonded to the soul and memory. Such a theory, obviously, takes very seriously the power of images, giving them a special efficacy in any person's life. Miles explains this power well:

> This strong visual experience was formulated negatively as the fear of contamination by a dangerous or "unsightly" visual object or positively as belief in the miraculous power of an icon, when assiduously gazed upon, to heal one's disease. Popular beliefs and practices support the conclusion that medieval people considered visual experience particularly powerful for one's good or ill. The persistence of belief in the "evil eye" from classical times to the sixteenth century and beyond is a good example. The evil eye was thought of as a maleficent visual ray of lethal strength. A person who had the evil eye reportedly could touch and poison the soul or body of an enemy. The only protections against the evil eye were making the sign of the cross, keeping one's body thoroughly covered against the baleful touch, and, especially, never meeting the eye of such a person; to do so would be to connect the two visual rays and allow the evil ray direct access to one's soul.[26]

If this understanding of vision seems to a modern person to exaggerate the power of visual experience, it also provides a corrective to an opposite exaggeration in our own approach to the visual. Understanding well the physical aspects of vision, we can reduce vision to those aspects, thus tending to overlook the psychological, moral, and spiritual aspects of visuals, almost the way the film and television industries do. Miles warns, "Despite the constant bombardment of images for commercial and entertainment purposes..., modern people prefer to think of themselves as disengaged voyeurs."[27] The disengagement is illusory. The evidence of studies like the Eron-Huesmann one and the claims of articulate analysts like MacKinnon regarding the influence of visuals on behavior suggest we attend to the insight of medieval people and be more suspicious of any assumption that visuals do not affect us. Miles's third difference between medieval and modern appropriation of images has to do with context, but I will save her explanation of this matter for the following chapter, where I deal with the functioning of metaphoric images.

Miles's warnings about the potential destructive power and MacKinnon's about the actual brutalizing power of iconic images are actually about the possibility of cultural pollution. If we define pollution as that which infects and eventually causes deterioration in life-fostering processes, we might be able to see an analogy between ecological pollution and cultural pollution. Cultural pollution involves the despoiling of the chain, not of bio-generative processes, but of the processes of human signification, of human meaning. Like ecological pollution, cultural pollution is silent and difficult to detect but proceeds to cause a breakdown of the processes of human valuing and understanding. Though it is not unusual for critics to complain of noise pollution or even of visual pollution of the countryside through the proliferation of roadside signs, very few have noted that cultural pollution, like biological pollution, comes to reside within us.[28] Distorted or false images of life, values, wants, and desires do not pollute our environment of meaning in some way outside us. Unless we work vigorously to contain them or to counter them, we easily become hosts to these distorted messages.

The full significance of iconic images cannot be gotten at from attention to the content of images only. Besides having their own content, images function in contexts. In the following section, dealing with the possibility of contesting images, I will treat context from one of its most comprehensive angles, that of ideology. Here I suggest a possible classification of two kinds of contexts that may help us think about the relevance of when, where, how, and why we actually see what we see. As products of someone or some system, images have one kind of context. As we actually encounter them in specific situations, they have another kind of context. Let me explain.

If we examine the contexts of images *as products,* produced out of certain interests and offered to achieve certain purposes, we see that they simultaneously partake of more than one context. We could them classify these as *immediate, intermediate, and distant.* The immediate context is that of the interests or intentions of those who produced the images. For most images, especially electronically communicated ones, in our society the immediate context is that of *selling.* Behind the production process is the desire to market something, and that marketing process finances the production of these images. I watch a narrative on television; the immediate purpose of the drama is as a vehicle to sell me something. I suggest that this context is functioning even in so-called non-commercial TV. Those who produce the images have agendas or interests that precede the specific character of the images themselves.

The *intermediate* context, unlike the immediate one of interests, is tied to the nature of the visuals themselves. The intermediate purpose of a narrative is to please or to inform. That of a picture would also be to inform, to portray, and/or to please. The *distant* context is that of the culture out of which the visual comes. This context sets the possibilities of expression found in any image. The photograph was impossible to conceive of before the development of scientific technology in the nineteenth century, and impressionism in painting was the result of the influence of the photograph on the craft of painting. Any image is part of an idiom that sets the boundaries of how the image can be conceived. Presented here in its unfinished state, this schema may help us be more reflective about the functioning of visuals, since the context of any visual affects us variously but certainly.

If there is a context to images as products, there is another *context of our seeing* or watching the images. Here again we have at least three simultaneous contexts. The *immediate context* is found in the purpose of watching, that is, the interests behind the watching. One person might watch television, say, as a way of inducing sleep at night time. Another, drained by work of psychological energy, might watch because conversation or reading is too taxing. Still another could watch in a search for information she or he considers important. Thus, the immediate context of the watching seems to be much more varied than the immediate context of the visual understood as product.

The *intermediate context* of the watching or seeing is found in the actual physical environment of the watching. Is one watching television in a bar while conversing with others; at home while children are playing in the same room or nearby; in sumptuous surroundings or in a prison cell? Does one read the glossy fashion magazine in the leisure of one's favorite chair or in a soup line, having just found the magazine on the street? To see David Lean's *Lawrence of Arabia* on a huge theater screen (in a quiet theater) is very different from seeing the same work on a home video screen. Many times the immediate and intermediate contexts can be hard to separate, such as when one sees a picture while leafing through a magazine in a barber shop or a dentist's office as a way of using up time — or while searching methodically in some other locale for erotic stimulation.

The *distant context* of seeing or watching is found in the life structure of the person doing the watching. The overall pattern of one's life at a particular time is what shapes the immediate environment and even the purpose of watching. Parents of very young children who have seized a rare opportunity to view a serious film in a theater have a very different distant context of that seeing than do the teens sitting near them, preoccupied more with each other than with the film. If the visual product has its effect on us, so do these simultaneous contexts in which we encounter the visual. They merit our attention. This classification may help us recognize the full complexity of visuals as they affect us.

## Critiquing or Contesting Images: Single-frame Images

My basic point in this examination of images is certainly not that all images function in a negative way but that we should be able to think about them, understand how they work, and make judgments about their value. Some will ask if such a process of judgment does not ruin the simple enjoyment to be found in viewing a film, a television program, or in listening to music. Why do we have to take everything apart through analysis? This is a serious question. It is true that analysis could become a compulsion never opening onto the kind of delight which is the core of true appreciation. My answer looks to how aesthetic enjoyment is enhanced. Does nuanced understanding heighten enjoyment or diminish it? When judgment is enhanced, is enjoyment diminished? Does the person trained to play the violin or viola have, when attending an opera, a lessened enjoyment of the opera? In other words, does the fact that a person is able to pay enhanced attention to what is happening among the strings and hear with sharpened judgment sounds many in the audience never consciously hear, add to or detract from that person's enjoyment of the opera? I would say that such a nuanced understanding adds.

Enhanced attention and enhanced judgment add to enjoyment, while making it more complex. One's enjoyment becomes tied to judgments of more and less, of better or lesser artistry, and so forth. So, too, would the skills of a person who had studied orchestration, or voice, or conducting, or set design. For that matter, a child who had some skill in gymnastics would bring it to her enjoyment of circus acrobatics. By bringing judgment actively into play, these skills make enjoyment more nuanced and heightened. Enjoyment can operate at various levels. Children enjoy slapstick almost universally but easily miss the point of wit. Adults should be able to give themselves over to slapstick and enjoy it, but also appreciate wit. Perhaps that is why some children might enjoy equally the Three Stooges and Laurel and Hardy, while adults prefer the latter for their ability to wed slapstick to an element of wit. "I enjoyed it" is not the last word of aesthetic appreciation. One could apply similar reflections to baseball or gardening.

Understanding, questioning, and even contesting visuals are not so easy, since visuals do not "work" the same way as the spoken or written language we call discourse. In the next several paragraphs I will deal with four features of single-frame pictures that should be of help in addressing these images. First, in discourse we make claims, assertions, raise questions, give commands, but pictures function differently. They do not make assertions or give commands or raise direct questions.[29] Think of handing a picture to ten different persons and asking each what the picture is saying; you could easily have ten different answers. Richard Moran offers an apt example to show how pictures are different from assertions. Say religious people find a certain picture offensive and want to oppose it. There is no way of merely "quoting" the picture to get at what its offensiveness is. You have to show the picture itself. But if you reproduce the picture to comment on it and show why it is offensive, you have in effect repeated the very thing you found objectionable. Someone's offensive words, however, can be quoted and critiqued without repeating the kind of offense the words originally had. The inverted commas are a way of saying, "These words are not mine; they are someone else's and from a particular context." You cannot quote a picture in this way because the picture "means" differently.

Though not making assertions, pictures do, however, present *versions*, a second feature I want to advert to. After all a picture is not just *of something*; it is *by someone*, and it offers that someone's point of view. As MacKinnon points out so well, that person wants us to look at some reality and to see it from a certain angle. A third feature of pictures is the visual context in which a particular picture appears. Here I use context in a more literal way than in the last section, where I tried to schematize the context of visuals in general. The context "frames" the picture and invites comments or comparisons, but in an indirect way, more similar to metaphor than to direct assertion. A picture of a teen-aged girl in a fashion magazine for teens where the focus is heavily on appearance has a different import from a picture of a teen in a newspaper news story. Sometimes the context involves written text commenting on the picture and leading us to interpret it in a particular way. A picture often takes its meaning from the way it is juxtaposed with other pictures, "absorbing" in a sense the meaning of the other pictures.

During the 1988 U.S. presidential campaign, George Bush attacked his opponent, Michael Dukakis, by juxtaposing pictures of Dukakis with those of a convict who raped while on furlough from a prison in Dukakis's state. Dukakis's image was intended to absorb, in an implicit way, the unfavorable connotations of the convict and his deed. The context of pictures invites comparisons or connections that need to be thought about if they are not to affect us in manipulative ways. If what frames a picture is significant to how it means, a fourth feature, the juxtaposition of elements within the frame itself, is equally so. Often enough, pictures are composed with these internal elements arranged for careful effect. That arrangement is open to analysis, as Erving Goffman has so astutely shown.[30]

In order to contest a picture, one must deal with its version of reality and make a judgment about its acceptability or unacceptability. Noticing what that version is and why one can or cannot accept it represents a special skill of cultural agency. Women see that an entire class of ads in magazines depict women exclusively at household tasks or in subservient positions, if not subservient roles,[31] and they begin a boycott of the magazines or the products. Or, someone decides the consuming "life styles of the rich" are beneath attention and avoids ads and TV/film narratives centered on them.

In *Image as Insight,* Margaret Miles offers three steps, not necessarily sequential, for training oneself to choose and use single-frame images. In summary, these are:

1. Awareness of the messages one receives from the images with which one lives. (Suggested exercises: changing the pace at which one reads a newspaper to see, for example, how news photos function; comparing carefully texts and images.)

2. Visual training (after we have detected and dealt with our own compulsiveness in relation to media images and have come to notice and formulate the particular messages we receive from images and texts) to begin to ask questions about media messages. What is my daily fare of images and how do they help imagine my life for me?

3. Selection and development of a repertoire of images, chosen because they attract and because they help one envision personal and social transformation. This step involves making judgments about what one sees and selecting the images that are life-giving.[32]

From her consistent concern with context, Miles probably assumes these skills would be best developed within a community of discourse struggling to be faithful to some vision of reality. Barring such a group, few would come to such awareness or skills. Miles's steps are another example of the conviction that we can and must develop cultural awareness and agency with regard to visuals.

## Critiquing or Contesting Narrative Images

Narrative images (those in sequential frames) require special skills if we are to deal with them as cultural agents. A narrative presents a more nuanced and comprehensive rendition of reality than does a single picture. The narrative says this is how some people are; this is how they feel and act in certain situations. If any icon invites mimesis, then imaged narratives have special influence. Presented to us graphically is not just how we could look but how we could behave in entire patterns of action. The earlier-cited statistical evidence that dramatizations of suicide on television accounted for an increase of twenty suicides nationwide is but one example of the mimetic power of visual narratives.

Helena Sheehan's approach to these narratives is one I have found especially helpful. Sheehan claims most people have no coherent criteria by which to judge television drama.[33] They either let the images wash over them, making only the most minimal judgments about what to watch, or if pushed to specify the reasons for what they do or do not watch, fall back on "I like/don't like it." Such people are not alone in their lack of criteria. They are joined by some schools of media studies which are unable to provide coherent criteria, preferring a pseudo-populist position that if many people watch it there must be something good in it. Such attitudes lead to accepting demographics as decisive criteria.

Sheehan's own approach — which I find as applicable to film as to television — is to examine the social, political, and economic conditions shaping the contexts of television production and consumption. She proposes two sets of criteria: aesthetic and ideological.[34] The former category has three inter-related sets of norms: production standards, quality of narrative, and dramatic criteria. Production standards offer criteria for judging the quality of "casting, performance, camera angles, soundtrack, lighting, locations, editing, wardrobe, and make up." She claims that the current tendency in international television is to stress the technical, formal, and financial aspects of television drama. Thus shoddy scripts can come to rely on "star" casting, exotic locations, fast-cutting, slick soundtracks, swashbuckling stunts, and high fashion.

In her view, all production considerations about visual style, pace, or performance should be subordinated to "evaluation of the script or narrative in terms of its basic human meaning." A dramatist or dramatic team can possess no attribute more fundamental than wisdom. Thus, before one can decide how to tell the story, one must first deal with the prior question "of whether it is a story worth telling."[35] A story worth telling does what all great art does: synthesizes and unifies human experience, cleanses perception, and illuminates what is hidden. Sheehan is saying that television should be judged by the norms by which the various dramatic genres should be judged: "scope, depth, integrity, authenticity, clarity, relevance, immediacy, rhythm, and resolution."

Recognizing that not every writer is gifted with great art, Sheehan does not suggest every television drama be perfect or embody a total vision. Her concern is rather with the overall drive in this medium: Is it toward totality and coherence or away from them? There can be an alternative drive toward decadence, fragmentedness, manipulation, and the lowest common denominator of human aspiration. In such a drive, dramatizations produce

> neither illumination nor catharsis. They have a ... mind-crowding, fragmenting, dissipating effect. They are decadent. They tell something about the temper of the times, but in a way that distracts attention from the true reality of the epoch, in a way that subverts the capacity to come to terms with it. They are seductively addictive, even to those who know better. ... Some enter more fully than others into the fantasies they construct, fantasies of macho aggression, fantasies of exploitative power and unearned wealth, fantasies of saccharine sentimentality and slushy sexuality.[36]

These considerations offer ample clues by which to begin the task of judging narratives, both televised and filmed. A religious dimension, judiciously brought to these criteria, may even sharpen judgment and aid in applying Sheehan's "ideo-

logical criteria." In the following chapter I will deal with
an aspect of ideological critique in examining the images or
lenses through which we see; my intention will be to help us
critique the iconic images we see all the time.

In proposing ideological criteria, Sheehan accepts Lukács's
position that the chief task of the critic is to shed light on
the relation between artistic creation and ideology. In this
view, ideology is a neutral term for the interconnected values generated by particular socio-historical conditions. Thus
ideology helps us understand a person's view of the world
as it is shaped by the particular social position from which
s/he perceives it. Ideology, like these individual world views,
does not just happen. It is embedded in the logic of a society's mode of production. Because it is embedded in the way
things are done, it gets inside people's heads. For Sheehan,

> an ideology provides the matrix of thought through
> which the world is perceived and conceived. Although
> it structures the very patterns of perception and con-
> ceptualization, it is itself usually neither perceived nor
> conceptualized. It often operates more in terms of im-
> plicit assumptions than explicit statements, shaping all
> that is seen, molding it within its framework, but re-
> maining itself unseen.[37]

Television and film drama has a powerful role in providing
that matrix of thought out of which the world is perceived.

In discerning and evaluating how this process works, Sheehan finds it necessary to deal with the overall patterns of
development in televised drama and to be able to trace the
"networks of assumptions embodied in the recurring images,
plots, settings, themes, genres and modes of characterization."[38] If we accept that every drama reveals something
about the forces operating in the society that produced it,
then we can examine the stories a society tells about itself
and to itself, for their world view, for information about how
the social order is structured, and about the rules it follows.
These stories either reinforce the social order or question it.
They can be examined for how they underscore the status

quo or challenge it. In calling for the critique of ideology, Sheehan applies to television drama critical perspectives already long-applied to literature.

An example of such help can be found in the following questions selected from a longer list in Helena Sheehan's book. These questions provide angles from which to probe the stories we see.

## Questions about the overall flow of programming:

- What stories are being told? By whom? Why?

- What alternative ways could these stories be told?

- What stories are not being told? Why not?

- How would we characterize and explain the standardized plots and patterns of resolution, the stereotypical modes of characterization (say, of women or men or of persons in certain roles, such as laborers or executives or religious personnel), and the stylized settings of the dramatic series we find on U.S. television?

- How could we explain the similarities and differences between these and those of, say, British or Canadian productions?

- How have any or all of these changed over the years? Why?

- What is the relationship between the patterns of development of these changes and the larger patterns for social change?

As I have pointed out here more than once, to these questions can be added religious criteria, which have great potential for critiquing any particular imagination of what life is all about. I will return to this matter in the following chapter.

Mark Crispin Miller, trained as a literary scholar, has applied similar norms to television and cinema in the U.S.

Miller calls for a step beyond "watching," i.e., a critical reading which allows us to judge visuals. In Miller's own words:

> To read is, in this case, to undo. Such a project, however, demands that we not just snicker at TV, presuming its stupidity and our own superiority. Rather, we need a critical approach that would take TV seriously (without extolling it), a method of deciphering TV's component images, requiring both a meticulous attention to concrete detail and a sense of TV's historical situation. Genuinely seen through, those details illuminate that larger context, and vice versa, so that the reading of TV contains and necessitates a reading of our moment and its past.[39]

The work of people like Miller and Sheehan provides, for those seeking to claim their own agency in the face of these electronic stories, important leads about how to engage in cultural analysis. A further skill in understanding how images work involves grasping how the images though which we see affect the images we actually see. To that matter I now turn.

## NOTES

1. I have commented on this problem in several places in *Youth, Gospel, Liberation* (New York: Don Bosco Multimedia, 1994), esp. pp. 62–72.

2. The example I have used here might seem to belie my own argument. In the course of the play, when the boy, Alan, repeats the jingles, the viewer wonders if there is unconscious, creative meaning to his choice of *these* particular jingles. However, they are never presented as anything more than inane babble, rote utterances symbolizing lack of touch with reality. See Peter Shaffer, *Equus* (New York: Avon Books, 1974).

3. Here I am taking the liberty of adopting "iconic images" to mean representational images. The matter of how to name visuals is actually quite complex, thanks to the classic (and complex) taxonomy of phenomena worked out by U.S. philosopher/mathematician Charles Sanders Peirce (1839–1914). Some commentators on religious art use icon in a quite specific way. Study convinces me that my usage here is acceptable. For some

recent work on various problems in classifying images, see Maria Lucia Santaella Braga, "For a Classification of Visual Signs," *Semiotica* 70, nos. 1/2 (1988): 59–78; Richard Moran, "Seeing and Believing: Metaphor, Image, and Force," *Critical Inquiry* 16 (Autumn 1989): 87–112; Tadeusz Kowzan,"Iconisme ou Mimetisme?" *Semiotica* 71, nos. 3/4 (1988): 213–26; M. R. Mayenowa, "An Analysis of Some Visual Signs: Suggestions for Analysis," in Jan van der Eng and Majmir Grygaer, eds., *The Structure of Texts and the Semiotics of Culture* (The Hague: Mouton, 1973), pp. 197–208.

Also, Charles Hartshorne and Paul Weiss, eds., *Collected Papers of Charles Sanders Peirce*, vols. 1 and 2 (Cambridge, Mass.: The Belknap Press of Harvard University Press, 1965), pp. 51, par. 92; 136–37, par. 230; 143–44, pars. 247–49.

4. An important analysis of the use of images in advertising is Raymond Williams, "Advertising: The Magic System," in *Problems in Materialism and Culture* (London: Verso, 1980), pp. 170–95.

5. See Neil Postman, "Engaging Students in the Great Conversation," *Phi Delta Kappan* (January 1983): 311.

6. Mark C. Miller deals with some of these stylistic shifts in "Hollywood: The Ad," *Atlantic Monthly* (April 1990): 41–68.

7. Some narratives — for example, Faulkner's *The Sound and the Fury* — while not having an immediately accessible coherence and plot sequence, gradually and finally prove to have exceptional coherence.

8. Postman, "Engaging Students," 314.

9. Helena Sheehan, *Irish Television Drama: A Society and Its Stories* (Dublin: Radio Telefís Eireann, 1987), p. 35. Two feminist studies of women's reactions to varied media bring out the contradictions in the actual effects of signifying forms: Lorraine Gamman and Margaret Marshment, eds., *The Female Gaze*, and Lisa A. Lewis, *Gender Politics and MTV*. See Elayne Rapping's review of these books, "Girls Just Wanna Have Fun," *The Nation* (27 August/3 September 1990): 206–9.

10. Here I am using mimesis exclusively to mean "imitation." Theoretical studies of mimesis would include other meanings. For a thorough such study, see Gunter Gebauer and Christoph Wulf, *Mimesis: Culture, Art, Society*, trans. Don Reneau (Berkeley: University of California Press, 1995).

11. Barbara Goldsmith, "The Meaning of Celebrity," *New York Times Magazine* (4 December 1983): 75ff.

12. In *Practicing Christianity: Critical Perspectives for an Embodied Christianity* (New York: Crossroad, 1988), Margaret Miles points out in several places the importance of visual representations in assisting prayer and the practice of asceticism in general down through the ages.

13. Catharine MacKinnon, "Pornography, Civil Rights, and Speech," *Harvard Civil Right–Civil Liberties Law Review* 20 (1985): 1–70, at 3.

See also her equally eloquent but more recent statement of these issues: *Only Words* (Cambridge, Mass.: Harvard University Press, 1993).

14. MacKinnon, "Pornography," pp. 16–17. Here and below I have underscored some of MacKinnon's phraseology I find particularly powerful.

15. Ibid., p. 18.

16. Ibid., p. 21.

17. See also Catharine A. MacKinnon, "Desire and Power: A Feminist Perspective," in Cary Nelson and Lawrence Grossberg, eds., *Marxism and the Interpretation of Culture* (Chicago: University of Chicago Press, 1988).

18. These examples are taken from the National Coalition on Television Violence, *Newsletter* 8, nos. 3–4 (July–August 1987), a special issue dealing with "Slasher" films and videocassette.

19. "Rising Brutality Complaints Raise Questions about New York Police," *New York Times* (6 May 1985), pp. A1 and B5.

20. Cited in Peter Plagens et al., "Violence in Our Culture," *Newsweek* (1 April 1991): 46–49; 51–52.

21. Janet Maslin, "Over the Top," *New York Times* (2 February 1987): C21.

22. I recommend Mark Crispin Miller's detailed analysis of the takeover of film by advertising in "Hollywood: The Ad."

23. This statement is true for a range of depictions, not just visual ones. Nicholas Luhmann, for example, explains that "since the 17th century, novels assume the role of providing instruction and orientation in affairs of the heart." See his *Love as Passion: The Codification of Intimacy* (Cambridge, Mass.: Harvard University Press, 1986), p. 11. His study, for its exploration of behavioral codes, has important implications for an understanding of culture.

24. Margaret Miles, *Image as Insight: Visual Understanding in Western Christianity and Secular Culture* (Boston: Beacon Press, 1985), p. 9.

25. Ibid.

26. Ibid., p. 7.

27. Miles's point here is admirably and entertainingly backed up by David Freedberg's well-informed and literate, *The Power of Images* (Chicago: University of Chicago Press, 1989). I have used his book to frame my own analysis in "The Material Conditions of Our Seeing and Perceiving," *New Theology Review* 7, no. 2 (May 1994): 37–59.

28. Raymond Williams uses the expression "cultural poverty" in his essay "Britain in the Sixties: The Long Revolution Analysis," and in some of his other writings, he describes cultural pollution without using the exact expression. For the above essay and another entitled "Culture and Technology," see *The Year 2000* (New York: Pantheon Books, 1983). Earlier, I noted Gustavo Gutiérrez's use of the term "cultural death" for the processes that kill the sources of spiritual hope of a people. See *We Drink from Our Own Wells* (Maryknoll, N.Y. Orbis Books, 1984), p. 10.

29. Here I am following Richard Moran, "Metaphor, Image, and Force," *Critical Inquiry* 16 (Autumn 1989): 101–3. Moran quotes and elaborates on C. S. Peirce's dictum that icons assert nothing. E. R. Gombrich makes a similar point in *Art and Illusion: A Study in the Psychology of Pictorial Representation* (New York: Pantheon Books, 1960): "Logicians tell us...that the terms 'true' and 'false' can only be applied to statements, propositions.... [A] picture is never a statement in that sense of the term. It can no more be true or false than a statement can be blue or green" (p. 67).

30. Erving Goffman's *Gender Advertisements* (New York: Harper Colophon Books, 1979) uncovers the importance of physical and emotional position in pictures, particularly in photographs. Where women and men appear together, women tend to have a diminished position. Goffman's introductory essays, pp. 1–27, are especially helpful.

31. Ibid.

32. Miles, *Image as Insight*, pp. 146–49. The context of these steps suggests to me that she means single-frame images.

33. *Irish Television Drama*, pp. 49–53, passim. Sheehan here agrees very much with similar comments about the lack of criteria made by Mark Crispin Miller in *Boxed-In: The Culture of TV* (Evanston, Ill.: Northwestern University Press, 1988), pp. 18–24.

34. Sheehan *Irish Television Drama*, pp. 54–70.

35. Ibid., p. 55.

36. Ibid., p. 63.

37. Ibid., p. 67.

38. Ibid., p. 69. In insisting on the importance of the history of a medium, Sheehan echoes a point often made by Williams.

39. Mark Crispin Miller, "The Hipness unto Death," in *Boxed-In*, p. 19.

*Chapter 6*

# METAPHORIC IMAGES AS SIGNIFIERS

## Understanding Metaphoric Images

In an image culture like ours we are all so "awash" in images that we can overlook the need to think about them. This was my claim in the previous chapter. Yet, the deeper problem is not that we look at images ceaselessly. It is that we look at reality through images. Here I am making an important distinction between the images we see and look at, iconic images, and those through which we see, which are metaphoric images. There is a function of the imagination that goes beyond the faculty of picturing absent objects and re-combining them into fantastic forms. Through this imaginal function, a person seeks analogies and metaphors by which to understand and name reality. Images in this sense provide us with analogous referents for knowing what things are like. In particular cultures, certain images provide the lenses through which to view reality. As with any kind of lens, we can easily forget that we are seeing through it. We do not see the lens exactly because we are so busy looking through it. Understanding this matter is crucial for cultural agency.

In a perceptive essay, theologian Charles Davis points out how metaphoric images "are the constitutive elements of the world of human meaning." The specific example Davis uses to illustrate such an image "through which we see" is the image of woman.

...The image of woman we have determines the social order and affects the lives of all of us. Image in
this sense is not just knowledge, such as is retailed
in anatomy, physiology, psychology, sociology or history. In some respects it precedes knowledge and guides
the knowing process. Again, an image selects items of
knowledge and arranges them into a pattern. An image
also includes a sense of choice of particular values. But
it is more than a value-judgment. The image of woman
is that set of facts and values which have been shaped
into a pattern so as to become a constitutive element in
the world of meaning of a particular society, culture or
civilization.[1]

Notice how this "image" of woman selects the aspects of
knowledge we choose to pay attention to but selects them
according to certain values and arranges them into a pattern.
In this sense, the image of woman has along with it a chain
of associations and expectations that are pre-conscious and
closely tied to feelings.

To illustrate how one's image of woman might function,
I use the following example, aware of its tendency to over-
simplify a complex reality. At the university where I teach
I find two very different images of woman in the minds of
the young men I meet. They, in turn, are continually evaluating the womanliness of the women they meet according
to criteria latent in these lens images. For some, a woman is
a coy, dependent, not over-bright individual with a particular "look," usually a look corresponding to fashion and to
anatomical calculations. Such a woman does not readily dis-
agree with a man, is apt to smile a lot in his presence, and
takes special pleasure in his sense of humor, that is, laughs
at his jokes.

Other men have a different image of woman. For them,
a woman is a self-directed adult, compassionate, reflective,
possibly witty, but in general able to meet other adults of
either sex on an equal footing. She is not better than men
but she is not less either. She does not hold that men and

women are the same, but she does hold they are equal. What we have here is more than simple personality preferences: we have lens images that select, arrange, and evaluate for us the significance of what we see and experience.

## Comprehensive Metaphors

To understand images more fully, we must recognize that underlying these lens images are even more basic images, which Gibson Winter calls comprehensive metaphors, functioning almost the way the eye does as the primal lens through which we see. If any lens tends to be taken for granted because we are busy seeing through it, all the more so the lens of the eye. So, too, are the comprehensive metaphors, which furnish coherence to our world and impose a fundamental pattern on all our experience, providing the underlying "sense of things" operative in a particular social order. Neither perceived nor conceptualized, they organize the basic coherence of the matrix of thought Helena Sheehan calls "ideology."

The comprehensive metaphor I wish to examine briefly is the domination-subordination metaphor, mainly because it is a metaphor that characterizes the consciousness of many in our society and because it also shapes the image of woman discussed above.[2] Domination-subordination thinking tends to break personal and social reality down into two groups: superior and inferior. Within this metaphor, the inferior need to be directed by the superior, need to be under their control or their domination. The domination-subordination metaphor, then, works out of a variety of dichotomies. There is the winners-losers dichotomy. In victory or winning, we get proof of superiority and of how rightful it is to dominate the beaten, defeated, or simply unequal group. The winner-loser dichotomy splits the superior from the inferior but also the stronger from the weaker.

It may be difficult, for example, to convince a young man unconsciously using this metaphor that because women's physical strength is of a different sort than men's, it

does not follow that women are necessarily poorer ath-
letes. Athletics is not so much about strength as about
skill. In the universe interpreted through the domination-
subordination metaphor, stronger means superior and dominant. These dichotomies — superior-inferior, winner-loser,
stronger-weaker — find their way into our everyday language, as when, in popular speech, certain individuals are
named "losers" and other "winners." Winners are those who
successfully dominate. They are the ones on top of things.

Though I have used the word "metaphor" here to describe the domination-subordination approach to reality, the
actual metaphoric elements are found in the spatial imagery
of those on top and those on the bottom, higher to lower,
superior to inferior. These metaphoric elements arise out of
the latent, almost hidden, underlying assumption about reality. In popular speech, we have a range of expressions about
being ahead or getting ahead or getting or having the advantage, as in a race. Of course, we speak of the arms "race"
where the Russians were once ahead and where we had been
ahead. Thus images from the playing field are transformed
to address the political arena.[3] "Clout" might be another
popular word that fits into domination-subordination thinking, combining imagery of the baseball bat with that of the
pre-historic club.

## Cultural Action and Metaphoric Images

Understanding how metaphoric images shape our world of
perception and interpret reality for us is an important step
in cultural action. Naming a particular lens image or comprehensive metaphor allows us to "see" and ponder how
it works. Only after such a step can one decide that the
metaphor may or may not be appropriate. Thus, naming a
particular reality, such as militarism, while at the same time
naming the metaphoric system of domination-subordination
supporting this reality, is a revolutionary act. To reject a
particular metaphor is, at some level, to reject the social

arrangements that metaphor supports. Recently, a substantial number of persons in our society have become astute in cultural action on metaphoric images. Leading them are feminists, who have understood well that liberation involves freeing oneself from the oppressor's imagination of life, which is supported by images.[4] Others skillful in this kind of cultural action are religious persons aware of the primal metaphors of their religious way and of how those images are at variance with so many of the metaphors of Western culture.[5] Still one can ask exactly how one person, say a member of a family, comes to name a metaphor, while other family members do not. The process whereby a metaphor assumes legitimacy needs more detailed explanation.

Here, Margaret Miles's third difference between medieval and modern experience of images is helpful. Medieval persons "saw" their *religious images*[6] in a context of public worship and devotional piety. Iconic images receive their coherence and power from their context in a wider, metaphoric image system. Applying this insight to medievals, Miles says:

> The individual viewer confronted the image as a member of an *interpreting community* [emphasis added here and below], and the image itself was also part of the architectural and liturgical presentation of an ordered cosmos of being, reality, and value. The position in the church building of the various depictions of Christ, the Virgin, saints, and scriptural events indicated their relative importance in the religious life of the community. . . .
>
> In addition, religious images were interpreted verbally and reinforced by the liturgy of the churches in which they appeared. In the sacraments conducted in this setting, priests reenacted the same cosmically significant activity, the same paradigmatic events that worshipers saw around them on walls, doors, and windows. The dramatic hieratic quality of the scriptural scenes of the stained-glass windows, spoken and sung in the lectionary of readings and hymns, was reflected

in the unity of word, object, and gesture in the sacraments. The *field from which to begin to understand the
meaning of any particular religious image to [medieval]
worshipers, then, is the occasion of public worship of
the Christian community.*[7]

Context is the field within which and from which images
take their power. If such a field can work in a positive way,
so it can work negatively, and one could find many negative
examples affecting people today. The reason iconic representations of violence are so acceptable and powerful today is
not simply that we live in a context where violence is depicted for us almost incessantly. These icons are supported
by the metaphoric language of domination-subordination by
which every chicanery, falsehood, or killing under military
auspices is legitimated in the name of "national interest."
The iconic and the metaphoric images become welded together in fostering violence the way they were for medieval
persons in fostering a religious vision.[8]

Miles's example of the images in the Middle Ages and my
own examples of violent images in our own time both show
the importance of context in maintaining a vision of reality. When I belong to a community of religious commitment,
one centered in following the Jesus who was criminalized
and victimized, and when our common commitment also
involves solidarity with the victims of society, then the
domination-subordination metaphor might become visible to
me. I may see how inappropriate for me — how unacceptable — is this cast of mind. Some virtuosos have an original
vision of reality, not fully embodied in any community, allowing them to counter the commonly accepted ways of their
time and lead others into their own vision, but they are rare.
Jesus and the prophets were such religious virtuosos. For
most of us, patterns of influence are more common. A child
lives in a family that embraces a commitment to common
humanity or a religious vision brought to bear on all features of reality. In the dialogue the parents initiate about the
images she sees and the images through which she sees, the

child can be given a means of evaluating the appropriateness of imagery.

Understanding the contextual field that lends power to metaphoric as well as iconic images is crucial for grasping how images work. Images, in conjunction with their validating contexts, tend to influence us with a power all the greater as we are less aware. However, this power can be broken. Images usually unnoticed in one context can become unacceptable when contested by images from another, more compelling, context, say a religious one. Christmas appeals to enhanced consumerism can be countered by insight into the Gospel infancy narratives and their theme of God's presence among the poor. Such a contestation is an almost natural process when one zone of meaning conflicts with another, though not all its outcomes are positive. For example, when religious meaning contests one's financial investments, financial security may be so compelling that religious claims are put to one side.

Of course, such a "natural" clash of images is not what I mean by cultural agency. Cultural agency is an intentional activity dealing with the specific problem of images in our day. If we live in the time of the sign, what is new is the proliferation of iconic images, not the proliferation of metaphoric images. We have always had metaphor as a way of interpreting reality; it is, as I have explained, embedded in the nature of human thought.

The process of cultural action on both kinds of images, iconic and metaphoric, calls for a special kind of awareness and intentionality. It involves first seeing the image, either iconic or metaphoric, with a kind of second look, *as an image*. Most people never get to this point. Images of both kinds are taken for granted. In regard to either kind of image, coming to see that one has a way of seeing involves a shift in consciousness, and for many this shift will be mediated through careful explanation. There is work here for those who would assist others in learning how to deal with the image systems of culture.

However, in addition to "seeing" the image, a second step

lies in evaluating the image, be it metaphoric or iconic. Someone is presenting me with this image to see or with this way of seeing. It is part of someone's agenda for me. Do I accept it? Is it appropriate? Is it congruent with my wider stance toward life? This second step will not be easily taken except as part of a community of commitment. The wider society presents me with a lens of domination-subordination with which to view reality. I tend to accept that version of reality very naturally, since it is presented to me as part of my "second nature," culture. Feminists provide a good example of a common commitment. When women commit themselves to human liberation and engage in that struggle together, forming a chorus with one another, they are more able to contest that "natural" way of looking at things.

## Learning to Contest Single Metaphors and Analogies

I have already noted that metaphor is a basic tool of thought and communication, but I have emphasized lens images and foundational metaphors. Here I wish to examine cultural agency on less comprehensive metaphors, those found in words or clusters of words and in analogies. In the "image culture," all persons, from governmental leaders to children, increasingly seek to explain themselves and their view of reality in metaphors. As already stated, my hypothesis is that because we are immersed in images, persons today tend, more so than before, to search out metaphors and analogies by which to explain what reality is like. Cultural agency is increased when persons can think about how metaphoric language and analogies work.

Most words we use in everyday language are based on a metaphoric foundation, and uncovering that base can enrich any word's meaning. When Daniel Berrigan was accused in court of conspiracy, he reflected publicly on the religious significance of the word, which had in it the prefix "con," meaning with, and the main element "spira," meaning breath. "Spira" is also the word from which the English "spirit," as in Holy Spirit, derives. Berrigan said that he and others who conspired were those who dared to breathe together and who invoked the common Spirit of Jesus. His astute understanding of metaphor allowed Berrigan to admit to conspiracy in the very moment of uncovering its religious base. Similarly, the word "reconciliation," an important religious word, takes new life when its underlying metaphors are disclosed. It combines three Latin words, "re," meaning "again"; "con," meaning with, as in conspire; and "celia," the Latin word for hair. The metaphor latent in this word suggests, then, that reconciliation involves a coming together again (re+con) of two persons who come to see so closely eye-to-eye that either their eyebrows or the lashes of their eyes (celia) meet. With its metaphoric underpinnings disclosed, reconciliation, like conspirator, reveals powerful nuances.

Words can have another sort of metaphoric quality when combined with other words in particular contexts. The following example illustrates how this happens:

> Your claims are *indefensible.*
> He *attacked every weak point* in my argument.
> His criticisms were *right on target.*
> I *demolished* his argument.
> I've never *won* an argument with him.
> You disagree? Okay, *shoot!*
> If you use that *strategy,* he'll *wipe you out.*
> He *shot down* all of my arguments.[9]

Each of these sentences is about argumentation, and each uses a war metaphor by which to speak about it. In such language, argument is being imagined by way of a war metaphor. If "the essence of metaphor is understanding and experiencing one kind of thing in terms of another,"[10] then shifting the metaphor can shift one's basic attitude toward the original matter, in this case, argument. What would happen to the way we conceive of argument if we imagined it, not as an act of war involving overcoming the other through destruction and even demolishment, but as a dance? Are there times when the metaphor of a dance is a more appropriate one for an argument than that of war? For instance, could an argument between lovers be better described in terms of dance, with each partner assuming differing positions but always with an eye to maintaining contact and to finding the position most expressive and enriching to both partners? Dance suggests partnership; war suggests enmity.[11]

## Inappropriate Metaphors: Some Examples

Selecting the right metaphor advances one's thought. Selecting an inappropriate metaphor subverts one's position. Likewise, to accept someone else's metaphor is to enter discourse on the terms selected by the other person. As one commentator puts it:

> Part of the dangerous power of a strong metaphor is its control over one's thinking at a level beneath that of deliberation and volition. In the mind of the hearer an image is produced that is not chosen or willed. The metaphorical assertion brings one to see something familiar *through* this image, framed by it.[12]

Ordinarily, these terms of the metaphor are acceptable to us either because we agree with them or because the metaphor is appropriate. However, it is possible to unwittingly accept a metaphor and then find oneself locked into the other's mindset or the imaginal patterns that underlie it. Sometimes a discussion will not go where we want it to go, because we do not notice that the terms of discussion have been pre-set by images we do not accept, but which, unnoticed, we cannot contest.[13] In this way, metaphor does not so much assert something as insinuate it, in the root meaning of the term, since metaphor worms into the conversation assumptions we might not accept if we were sharper in spotting them. Those metaphoric images pre-set the rules of discourse which will not go where one might want it to go until the rules themselves are contested. It is the equivalent of incorrectly buttoning a coat and finding all the subsequent buttons wrongly done. Understanding the metaphors underlying discourse is becoming more and more important in a time when political leaders are lacing political speech with metaphors that require skill if they are to be unlocked or even contested.

An instance of a discourse pre-set in imaginal assumptions occurred in the United States in 1983 when armed forces attacked Grenada, a tiny island in the Caribbean populated by 100,000 persons. The rationale for the invasion given by U.S. government officials was that the U.S. could not tolerate a communist regime "in its own backyard." This territorial metaphor bears scrutiny for its latent assumptions.

One could ask what the "backyard" metaphor means. For instance, why didn't these officials refer to Grenada as being in the U.S.'s "front yard"? In which direction does the U.S. "face"? Which border is front and which is back? If the U.S. sees the lovely Caribbean as the back of its house, one could ask why, especially since it puts the "front" facing an Arctic tundra, hardly an appealing front side. Could it be that we see North as preferable and South as somehow lesser? This raises a further question of the reasons a house faces a particular direction called the front and not in the opposite direction, which is called the back. What things do people put in their front yards and what things do they put in their backyards? How do they feel about either yard? Does the rubbish, for instance, go into the front yard or the back? I have not yet reached a conclusion in this probing of the metaphor, but the probing itself suggests certain assumptions and even biases in the selection of the metaphor. I see that the metaphor might not be appropriate. When I reflect further that *what is in our backyard, we own,* I finally decide that the metaphor is inappropriate and I reject it and the assumptions behind both it and the invasion. Apparently some governmental officials themselves saw the dangers in the metaphor because a few weeks after the inept assault, the Secretary of State began referring to communist regimes "in our neighborhood," a much less vulnerable image.

Here I have illustrated a form of cultural analysis through the examination of a metaphor for its inappropriateness. In a time when metaphors are being used more and more to shape the acquiescence of the public to various policies, this skill becomes more and more important as a skill in cultural agency. The ability to examine metaphors is an important conceptual skill, though it has not received a great deal of attention in the literature of education. One of the places I have found it exercised deftly has been in certain editorials appearing in the *New Yorker*.[14] I will examine two of these for the way they illustrate an awareness of the significance of metaphor and the art of contesting inappropriate metaphors and analogies.

The first editorial[15] comments on an interview in *Business Week* with Warren M. Anderson, chairman of Union Carbide, about a year after a leak at the company's chemical plant in Bhopal, India, killed 1,750 people within a few days, with many thousands blinded for life and over 60,000 adults unable to do a full day's work a year later. Commenting on the court cases that came from the disaster, Anderson said that at first he had "over-reacted," and went on to say, "This could drag on for five or more years. That's our way of life in America." He added, using a telling metaphor, "I'm not going to roll over and play dead." The editorial notes that in a later interview with a newspaper, Anderson took up this health metaphor again, saying, "Those first two months were tough, tough, tough. But my health is good. My blood pressure improved."

What I am noting in Weschler's wide-ranging commentary on corporate responsibility is the way he teases inappropriate language and images out of someone's statements for analysis and comment. Even without comment, highlighting inappropriate language and images, as Weschler does, can itself be a powerful way of exposing their inappropriateness. The editorial lets Anderson's remarks about his own health and "playing dead" speak for themselves and addresses only his "overreaction."

Weschler asks what it means to "overreact" to the destruction of human life and health that erupted in Bhopal. Could one "overreact" to such a horror? His answer is yes, say, if Anderson jumped out a window and killed himself. Or, could he have overreacted in a meaningless way, say, by quitting his job? Again, yes. However, would he have been overreacting had he announced he would spend the rest of his working life healing the devastating problems caused by the accident? In Weschler's view, such a statement would have not been overactive but appropriate, as appropriate as the million dollars Anderson actually donated to the relief effort. In his attempt to be fair to Anderson, Weschler suggests that by his "overreaction" Anderson may have been speaking of himself as a private person, a reaction he went beyond when he got in touch with his responsibilities as the head of a huge corporation. At this point Weschler's editorial proceeds to examine unflinchingly the moral responsibilities of corporations and their leaders.[16] In many instances these responsibilities involve facing squarely corporate guilt and responding with corporate reparation.

A fine example of working with metaphors with full awareness of how they function is from another of Weschler's *New Yorker* editorials, this one about the "peace talks" between the U.S. and the Soviet Union in the 1980s.[17] Weschler begins by noting how we tend to think in metaphors, which in turn lace our speech. For example the U.S.-Soviet talks between Ronald Reagan and Mikhail Gorbachev in the mid-1980s were called a chess match where each maneuvered for position. Finding this an odd metaphor for the arms race, Weschler asks what "victory" would actually mean in such a race or match with weapons of mass devastation of population and global environment. Atomic scientists use a quite different and more apt metaphor for the arms race — a clock whose minute hand is edging ever close to midnight: the end of the day.

Weschler's point is that we cannot help using metaphors though we must be careful to use appropriate ones. We have a responsibility to and for our metaphors. He illustrates this point with the speech Ronald Reagan gave before the

U.N. in 1985, after particularly futile and inconclusive arms talks with Gorbachev in Iceland left many people discouraged and frightened, including many diplomats throughout the world. The occasion was the fortieth anniversary of the founding of the United Nations, a moment many had originally hoped Reagan would use for announcing an important breakthrough in arms reductions. Alas, instead of progress, there had been a breakdown in negotiations. Reagan wanted to put a good face on the failed talks and to talk hopefully in the face of a disheartening impasse.

Reagan chose to compare the dangerous international arms race with the devastating Mexican earthquake of the month before, when nations from all over the world sent decisive help: financial aid, equipment, and teams of experts to help dig out the injured from the rubble. In what proved to be for many a very troubling end to his speech, Reagan focused particularly on a heart-wrenching scene that had been televised throughout the world, when workers digging in "a huge mount of rubble that was once the Juarez Hospital... heard a faint sound coming from somewhere in the heart of the crushed concrete..., and hoping beyond hope" uncovered three newborns miraculously still alive. Driving home his hopeful point he concluded, "Well, amidst all that hopelessness and debris came a timely and timeless lesson for us all. We witnessed the miracle of life." Reagan seemed quite pleased with his implicit comparison of the failed arms talks with the symbolic saving of the newborn infants from the rubble. Did he think he had made a key rhetorical coup, implying "all will turn out well"?

Whatever the president may have thought, Weschler notes that many diplomats in the audience had been hoping he would offer a response to Mr. Gorbachev's earlier proposals for dramatic reductions in strategic nuclear stockpiles, with at least some counter proposals of his own. These diplomats were looking for a glimmer of hope to the darkness offered by the huge arms build-up of the previous several years. What they got was this "untethered" metaphor.

The metaphor seemed untethered, that is, running loose and working in ways it was not supposed to, because, while it was meant as a palliative, in fact it seemed disturbingly sinister to many, who found in its reference to mounds of rubble and its suggestion of massive destruction, a chilling suggestion of events to come. Many throughout the world had already found in the Mexican earthquake a frightening, apocalyptic scenario, and this world leader's use of it at a moment in East-West tensions some found horrifying. Apart from its untethered quality, however, the reason Reagan's metaphor was *inappropriate* was that it tried to compare two realities not really comparable. The geological fault buried deep and pushing plates of the earth's crust upward, thereby causing devastation, was not properly compared with the surges and pulls of the leaders of the world's two great powers — and the possible devastation resulting from their unwillingness to compromise. In the one case there is a problem deep within the earth that can be monitored but not changed; in the other, any cataclysmic devastation would have come from human will.

In his conclusion, Weschler points out the vital difference between geology and history. History is shaped by human decisions, for good or ill. What happens in history human beings are responsible for, because they, at least to a degree, shape it. When arms reduction talks fail, they do so because of a lack of human will. In the end, salvaging the three babies from the hospital rubble, though a marvel of human survival, is not a triumph erasing the horrible catastrophe of that earthquake.

Skill in the analysis of metaphor involves seeing in whose interests a particular comparison is used, whether the comparison is apt, and why these two matters are brought together for comparison at all. This skill is one that can be developed and should be a basic conceptual tool in the time of the sign. I believe these matters can be explained to people so as to help them to think more clearly about their own positions. I have seen young people learn to re-name reality, adopting a new language to take them out of the language game, say, of the militarists in our own country who name weapons of destruction as peacekeepers. Also if I myself am conscious of my own metaphors and willing to talk about them as well as about the importance of proper naming, my students come to imitate my behavior. Model non-sexist language for students and many will come to see the point and be more discriminating in their own speech.

Understanding the connections between those images through which we see and those images we see and then working at interpreting both sets of images promises to open up many angles of cultural analysis and a dynamic kind of cultural agency.

# NOTES

1. Charles Davis, "Religion and the Sense of the Sacred," Catholic Theological Society of America, *Proceedings* 31 (1976): 87–105.

2. Though using domination-subordination as my example of a comprehensive metaphor here, I agree with Gibson Winter that at the deepest level, the most comprehensive metaphor of our time is the mechanistic metaphor, the metaphor of the machine. Actually, the domination-subordination metaphor is successful because it reinforces the metaphor of the machine. I found the first chapter of Winter's book of special help in understanding how comprehensive metaphors work. See Gibson Winter, *Liberating Creation: Foundations of Religious Social Ethics* (New York: Crossroad, 1981).

3. See George Orwell's treatment of this transformation in his brief essay, "The Sporting Spirit," George Orwell, *Selected Writings* (London: Heinemann, 1947), pp. 159–62.

4. A fine example of the contesting of images is the first two chapters of Starhawk, *Dreaming the Dark: Magic, Sex, and Politics* (Boston: Beacon Press, 1982).

5. One I consider a leader in this work is Joe Holland. See his essay "Linking Social Analysis and Theological Reflection: The Place of Root Metaphors in Social and Religious Experience," in James E. Hug, ed., *Tracing the Spirit* (New York: Paulist Press, 1983), pp. 170–91.

6. I stress "religious images" because, though we encounter our religious imagery differently today than did medieval persons, still, the basic process by which context lends credence and power to images is the same.

7. Margaret Miles, *Image as Insight: Visual Understanding in Western Christianity and Secular Culture* (Boston: Beacon Press, 1985), p. 8.

8. For a good analysis of assumptions tied to metaphoric elements in language, see Richard Barnet's examination of the language of national security used in statements of the national strategy of the United States. "Reflections: Rethinking National Strategy," *New Yorker* (21 March 1988): 104–14.

9. George Lakoff and Mark Johnson, *Metaphors We Live By* (Chicago: University of Chicago Press, 1980), p. 4.

10. Ibid., p. 5. The dance metaphor used below is from this same page.

11. Once when I was teaching about conflict resolution in a class on marriage, a student objected that my approach was unrealistic and not usable by him in his real-life situation with his girlfriend. I asked him to role play with me about a real-life, specific issue. We went back and forth several times as I tried to understand his position and asked him to consider mine. Finally, at one point he stopped and said, "If I continue with this, then I'll lose." I then asked him why he applied the logic of football or basketball in dealing with the one he loved and hoped to spend a lifetime with. It seemed to me he was using the wrong metaphor.

12. Richard Moran, "Metaphor, Image, and Force," *Critical Inquiry* 16 (Autumn 1989): 90–91.

13. In a passage that sheds light on metaphor and argument, philosopher Alisdair MacIntyre explains the relatedness of theory and idiom:

> Theory and idiom are to some significant degree inseparable. Insofar as I try to deny your theory, but continue to use your idiom, it may be that I shall be trapped into presupposing just what I aspire to deny. And correspondingly the more radical the disagreement over theory, the larger the possibility that each party will find itself misrepresented in the idioms of its rivals, idioms which exclude rather than merely lack the conceptual resources necessary for the statement of its position.

Alisdair MacIntyre, *First Principles, Final Ends, and Contemporary Philosophical Issues* (Milwaukee: Marquette University Press, 1990), p. 5.

14. When I originally read these editorials, I had no idea who had written them. Only later did I find out that all the editorials that had impressed me — many more than the two reviewed here — were written by Lawrence Weschler. Readers should note that I have paraphrased both editorials.

15. "Notes and Comment," *New Yorker* (13 January 1986): 17–18.

16. For a similar probing of inept language, this time from a South African Governmental Minister of Law and Order, see "Notes and Comments," *New Yorker* (8 September 1986): 27–28.

17. "Notes and Comment," *New Yorker* (11 November 1985): 35–36.

*Chapter 7*

# HEGEMONY AND THE POSSIBILITIES OF CONTESTATION

So far I have tried to set out the problem created over seven or eight decades by the shift of the material conditions of communications. Increasingly, the electronic means of communication have been able to create for large numbers of persons a world of meaning they tend to consume, not create or even engage with creatively. My purpose in looking at this problem has been to foster what I have called cultural agency: the ability first to think about how meaning is created, in whose interests it is created, and what sort of rendition of reality it is; and secondly, the ability to make judgments about the meaning presented us, using aesthetic, ideological, and religious criteria. My view is that the skills of cultural analysis can be accessible to large numbers of persons who can learn to see how they see. Now at the end of my study, I wish to go back and re-examine the matter of agency.

Embedded in this final chapter are a series of questions to rethink: What difference will cultural analysis make? Are the forces controlling the culture industries so powerful that in fact very little can be done about the situation? If a handful of persons are empowered to think about culture and its processes, what difference will their awareness make when so many others ingest culture so unthinkingly? Most importantly, could it be possible that my description of culture

here and my approach to cultural analysis might actually discourage cultural agency? This last question was raised for
me by a reader of an early draft of my work. There are
ways of describing a problem, he warned, that ultimately do
not empower us to face the problem but instead convince
us not much can be done. This happens when a problem
is presented as so massive and possessing such complete
power that it can be understood but not countered or even
acted on.[1] Such a comment on my own approach here set
me to revise my work but also to think about the problem of empowerment in the face of social situations of great
complexity.

The task of explanation, as Clifford Geertz reminds us,
is not to reduce the complex to the simple but rather to
substitute "complex pictures for simple ones while striving
somehow to retain the persuasive clarity that went with the
simple ones." The advancement of understanding becomes
possible through a progressive complication of what once
seemed an attractively simple problem. In the long run, such
an advancement substitutes the "involved but comprehensible for the involved but incomprehensible."[2] The problem I
concern myself with in this chapter is that of making social
reality not only *comprehensible but actionable.* In making
such a distinction, I realize that comprehension itself is the
seminal form of action. For action to move beyond a neural
physical response and become a human achievement, it must
fuse intelligence and energy. Lacking human attention and
understanding, no advance of action is possible, which is one
reason despots work so hard at strategies for drawing attention away from their misdeeds. Of course there is always the
possibility that a complex problem well-understood could be
met with simplistic action, inadequate to the true nature of
the problem or giving the illusion of doing something significant.[3] On the matter of oversimplification, we have, then,
two possibilities: the oversimplification of the *comprehension* of the problem but also of the *action* needed for coping
with the problem. Based on these clarifications of attention as a form of action, the question here remains whether

there are explanations that inhibit the kinds of action beyond attention-as-action.

The study required for writing this book introduced me to several critiques of culture, most quite convincing, that presented the problem of one or another dimension of contemporary persons-in-society in graphic but depressing terms, and without offering lines of action for countering the situation they described. Were they empowering or the opposite, fostering inaction? Of course, there were other critiques claiming the problem capable of being faced and countered. About these I could ask: Were their proposals for action wisely made or inept? Here I wish to examine a series of critiques for their potential role in empowering or dispiriting, but also as a way of getting at the question of cultural agency once more and in greater depth. I will present first those critiques that seem to present cultural dilemmas without proposals for action and then move to those offering such proposals. Finally, I wish to re-examine the question of cultural action from a religious perspective.

## Baudrillard's World of Simulation

Jean Baudrillard is a French social philosopher who has been trying to describe the particular character of contemporary culture. Most recently, he has been struggling with the structure of communications in a world dominated by electronic media. Baudrillard's analysis is, to say the least, "totalizing," as Mark Poster notes in his introduction to his collection of the philosopher's writings.[4] Indeed, I, myself, find his descriptions of what is happening today a kind of dizzying mental free fall but also stimulating as a way of naming what many people are actually living.

For Baudrillard, a key aspect of our former industrial society was production, whereas in today's post-industrial society, it is simulation. Industrial production was able to crank out in series products that were exact replicas of one another, first through human-labor assembly lines and later, through automation. These replicas were, in a sense, simulations but in a qualitatively different degree than today's simulations. In the current world of simulations, all reference to the real has been replaced. Now models create a "real" that has no true reference to reality or to origins. Baudrillard uses an allegory of a Jorge Luis Borges tale to ground his idea. In this story, the map-makers of the Empire draw a map that exactly details its territory. As the Empire deteriorates, so does the map, and in the end only shreds of it are found rotting in the deserts, actually returning to the very earth the map had represented. Unlike the map, representation today no longer follows on and represents a reality such as the Empire's territory. Today, instead, the map precedes and creates the Empire. Indeed to make the fable applicable to today, the territory itself, the reality, would have to rot in shreds, not the map; for today it is the real that one finds here and there in bits and vestiges.

When I first read this essay by Baudrillard I was sitting quietly trying to get behind his somewhat obscure point. My phone rang and I answered it. There was a voice, but no person was on the line. A reproduction of a voice exhorted me to buy something. Music and a cheering crowd in the background had also been simulated to add a certain character to the voice of the person on the phone who was not really there. This phone message helped me understand Baudrillard's claim that

> present-day simulators try to make the real, all the real, coincide with their simulation models.... Something has disappeared: the sovereign difference between them that was the abstraction's charm.... [Today] the real is produced from miniaturized units, from matrices, memory banks and command models — and with these it can be reproduced an indefinite number of times.... It is a hyperreal.[5]

Baudrillard would surely have understood the former New York City police inspector's claim, cited previously, that many officers are having their job imagined for them by film and TV renditions of police and are performing more in that mode than in the way they were initially trained.

The significance of the new time of simulation can be seen in the difference between dissimulation and simulation. To dissimulate is to make believe one does not have what one actually does have, or does not know what one, in fact, does know. The act of dissimulation implies a presence: what one really has or really knows is present but not admitted. To simulate, however, is to make believe one has or knows what in fact one does not. Thus it implies an absence: what one pretends to have or know is really not there.

Yet the matter is complicated by the fact that to simulate involves a step beyond feigning or make believe. The case of feigning illness makes this clear, because to simulate an illness one must *produce some of the symptoms* of illness, a pretense that threatens the difference between "true" and "false," between "real" and "imaginary." In contemporary society, Baudrillard claims, the reality principle disappears. I presume that for a philosopher like Baudrillard, this possibility of masking the difference between true and false has chilling consequences. Indeed, his alarm appears to me to underlie all his writings I have read but is hinted at in the following passage:

> Since the simulator produces "true" symptoms, is he or she ill or not? The simulator cannot be treated objectively either as ill, or as not ill. Psychology and medicine stop at this point, before a thereafter undiscoverable truth of the illness. For if any symptom can be "produced," and can no longer be accepted as a fact of nature, then every illness may be considered as simulatable and simulated, and medicine loses its meaning since it only knows how to treat "true" illnesses by their objective causes.[6]

The example he uses to illustrate the character of simulation today is Disneyland in Southern California. Here he finds a quasi-religious celebration of "real" America. Though the park is a world of fantasy, it lays out in miniature an objective profile or map of the United States. Both the map and the "reality" it supposedly stands for are illusions. Here in miniature and comic-strip form, the nation's values are exalted, but in an infantalized mode. According to Baudrillard, Disneyland is a double kind of simulation since it aims

> to make us believe that the rest is real, when in fact all of Los Angeles and the America surrounding it are no longer real, but of the order of the hyperreal and of simulation. It is no longer a question of a false representation of reality (ideology), but of concealing the fact that the real is no longer real, and thus of saving the reality principle.... It is meant to be an infantile world, in order to make us believe that the adults are elsewhere, in the "real" world, and to conceal the fact that real childishness is everywhere, particularly among those adults who go there to act the child in order to foster illusions of [regarding] their real childishness.[7]

He goes on to name the various "imaginary stations" surrounding Los Angeles: Enchanted Village, Magic Mountain, Marine World, nuclear power stations, and film studios.

Baudrillard applies this same analysis of what I will call "the double illusion" (what we call illusion fosters a chain of illusions in ways we do not recognize) in other places in his writings. The Watergate scandal, for example, had the effect of allowing the law to seem to triumph, thus disguising the fact that capital truly runs the country. However, capital, immoral and unscrupulous, needs a moral superstructure behind which to hide. And so, when the *Washington Post* journalists helped regenerate public morality and the rule of law, they propped up the very illusions that allowed capital to run free once more. From this sort of analysis there seems no escape. All are trapped in a system that cannot be contested.[8]

Baudrillard would seem to deny all real agency in his description of the way people are coded into a simulated order. In a commentator's words, for Baudrillard responses [of citizens] are structured into a binary system of affirmation or negation: every ad, fashion, commodity, television program, political candidate and poll presents a test to which one is to respond: Is one for or against? Do we want it or not? Are we for X or Y? In this way, one is mobilized in a coded system of similarities and dissimilarities, of identities and programmed differences. . . . The political upshot of his analysis seems to be that everything in the system is subject to cybernetic control and that what appears to be oppositional, outside of, or threatening to the system are really functional parts of a society of simulations.[9]

If followed to their logical conclusion, these ideas seem to say that persons in society, in whatever combination of group effort, are incapable of social action. Only conformity is possible because the masses are satisfied with spectacle. Baudrillard repeats this idea in many places.

In an essay on the relation of the masses to media,[10] he finds in these masses "a radical anti-metaphysics," a radical lack of will by which they choose not to will, not to decide about themselves or their world, not to wish, not to desire. Instead, they hand over the responsibility for all these activities to someone else — not a special surrogate but anyone — who will wish, desire, and decide for them. They prefer to rely on publicity-type information to offer them a choice or on the political class to order things for them.

What can I say about this sort of critique? How helpful is it? At the same time I found it both insightful and discouraging, describing an almost hopeless situation. Frequently Baudrillard's insights have come back to me, helping interpret some aspect of contemporary culture; yet, at other times, on re-reading him, I was convinced he was a nihilist. My suspicion, in the end, is that his essays are meant as kinds of philosophical morality plays, mirrors held up to us to help us see and judge the absence of moral judgment and action in our time. I suspect Baudrillard intended my conflicting responses as a way of keeping a problem conflictual and thus open to further thought. From this angle, I find his critique valuable. Baudrillard never strays far from the humanist philosopher concerned about goodness and truth. If, at a conceptual level, his vision is dizzying in its negativity, at an emotional level, however, I find a call to a new way of paying attention to what is happening and a new series of tasks to help others pay similar attention. His position that culture itself fosters today an immobility incapable of being disrupted caused me to reflect deeply and resolve to work to help others see the problem. Again, perhaps such was Baudrillard's intent.

## The Culture of Surface:
## Corroboration of Baudrillard's Position

If Baudrillard seems to present his account of the contemporary world in terms offering few clues to countering the situation, his basic insight about the unreality of reality is borne out by several commentators working independently of one another in the U.S. Barbara Goldsmith reports a Manhattan dinner party whose celebrity guests included a U.S. Senator, an embezzler, a woman said to spend $60,000 a year on flowers, the host of a talk-show, the chief executive officer of one of the nation's largest corporations, a writer who had settled a plagiarism suit, and a Nobel laureate. Goldsmith points out that such an assemblage blurs the distinction between fame and notoriety, between talent and its lack, between accomplishment and merely being well-known, between heroes and villains. What these persons had in common was celebrity status. They all gave an "image" or impression of some quality: wealth, success, heroism, glamour, leadership, danger. When such synthetic personalities become heroes and heras, it is a sign a society is absenting itself from the ethical judgment needed for social health. Almost echoing Baudrillard, Goldsmith writes, "We no longer demand reality, only that which is real seeming."[11]

Since the characteristics of a society are found in those

it celebrates, an increasing lack of concern about the qualifications of these celebrities has ominous portent. Beyond the preference it shows for synthetic persons vicariously acting out a society's noblest and basest desires, it portends a preference for illusion over reality. In a vein again similar to Baudrillard, Goldsmith says:

> In today's highly technological world, reality has become a pallid substitute for the image reality we fabricate for ourselves, which in turn intensifies our addiction to the artificial. Anyone who has attended a political convention or a major sporting event knows that watching the proceedings on television, where cameras highlight the most riveting moments, then replay and relate them in similar situations, provides us with more stimulating and complex perceptions than being there does.
>
> Next year's visitors to the Grand Canyon need not see it. One mile from the boundary will be a $5 million complex where they will be able to view a film of the way the Canyon looks during all four seasons and take a simulated raft ride through artificial rapids.[12]

And so the mechanically recorded and technically altered reality has greater value than the actuality. Kennedy Fraser, a journalist specializing in fashion, picks up the same theme from her own perspective — but only after stepping out of her usual role of commenting about the fashion industry and turning to critique fashion itself.

Fraser finds that, in its deepest sense, fashion is about something more significant than couture or frivolities of taste. Neither named nor noted, it is rather "the lens through which our society perceives itself and the mold to which it increasingly shapes itself."[13] Hidden and unacknowledged, this mental kind of fashion needs to be brought into the light and evaluated. Mental fashion has much in common with the frivolous, pirouetting, old kind of fashion — that of dress: both hold appearances to be of greater significance than substance. "Among [their] shared limitations are fickleness, a preoccupation with descrying the will of the majority in order to manipulate it or pander to it, and a concern with the accumulation or protection of power and profit." Though often passing itself off as rebellious, fashion actually works to support power: "to think or act for reasons of fashion in any given field is to support that field's established centers of power."

Fraser is describing the nose for trend in the search for "the right stuff," not in the sense of the correct clothing styles but rather of the right ideas, the right interests, the right values, even the right spiritual concerns. Many infected by this kind of fashion are unaware what a "skilled master of enthusiasm" they have leading them. Even those who should be fostering quality, individuality, and the ability to reflect — writers, critics, artists, editors, and so forth — are apt to present ideas and facts as trendy commodities. They help society hand itself over to trend and style as worthy guides of the human project. Fraser warns that when fashion becomes the framework for perception, it warps not only perception but any reasonable picture of the world:

> The greatest drawback of an over fashionable perception is that fashion is concerned, virtually by definition, with surfaces, images, appearances.... When the mind surrenders itself to fashion, the first casualty is objective judgment — which is, to all intents, the mind itself. Fashionable perception is incapable of discerning any fixed truth about an object or event.[14]

Intelligence, on the other hand, demands honest, disinterested distinctions, "born of an isolated, dogged, unfashionable side of the mind — a sort of gawky mental provincialism." Ironically, the market for mental fashion is especially vital among the college-educated who, having tasted intellectual activity, are now nostalgic for the literary enthusiasms of studenthood. As a result, society patterns itself on fashion, with serious political and cultural consequences.

I choose to present at this point Goldsmith's and Fraser's ideas — found in two relatively short essays — because they reinforce Baudrillard's main positions. But the ideas themselves represent a form of cultural critique that describes a current situation in enough detail to engage one's concern about it, but without offering explanations of just how the situation has arrived at its current state or what might be done to counter it. This kind of critique seems to me to be insightful but incomplete, needing more evidence, analysis, and causal connections to help us think more deeply about the situation. Still, it is very important. My own study of culture was undertaken in part because of interest stimulated by Fraser's and Goldsmith's descriptions of the problems of celebrity and of the fashionable mind.

A third commentator on the phenomenon of illusion and surfaces in contemporary culture is Stuart Ewen, especially in *All-Consuming Images: The Politics of Style in Contemporary Culture.*[15] Ewen claims that style is all about surfaces, "mouth-watering" ones presented as material objects promising to free a life of the daily humdrum, allowing it to float beyond the terms of the real world. "Without ever saying so explicitly, the media of style offer to lift the viewer out of his or her life and place him or her in a utopian netherworld where there are no conflicts, no needs unmet; where the ordinary is — by its very nature — extraordinary."[16] The value of Ewen's book is that he suggests the historical background for understanding how style came to so function today and then analyzes specific features of its actual functioning. If Baudrillard, Goldsmith, and Fraser offer important descriptions of the contours of this cultural territory of illusion, Ewen offers a detailed map and geological history. His map helps us know the specifics of the territory and the workings of style.

Ewen notes that while style makes statements, it has no convictions. Citing an ad for jeans, he shows how the supposed "egalitarianism" of the product is underscored by information given about the blond, blue-eyed model: "Waitress, Bartender, Non-professional AIDS Educator, Cyclist, Art Restoration Student, Anglophile, Neo-Feminist." Ewen comments: "In the world of style, ideas, activities, and commitments become ornaments, adding connotation and value to the garment while they are, simultaneously, eviscerated of meaning."[17] Of course also eviscerated are Fraser's honest, disinterested distinctions, born of dogged, unfashionable, gawky mental provincialism. Instead, "modern style speaks to a world where change is the rule of the day, where one's place in the social order is a matter of perception, the product of diligently assembled illusions."[18] Ewen cautions us against seeing style as only a matter of subjectivity. We must, like Kennedy Fraser, understand how it is created to support the centers of power in social, political, and economic life.

Ewen's survey of the roots of contemporary style goes back to the rise of the profit economy in medieval towns. As capital became a mobile form of wealth, merchants came to mimic the consumption practices of the nobility, which at first included elaborate clothing. The new merchant-class wealth looked to a variety of objects and products that might signal the status their wealth deserved. As style became something one could purchase, a new commerce in appearances emerged. Entrepreneurs devised ways of reproducing desirable books, such as lavishly illustrated Books of Hours, so as to make them more widely accessible to those who craved the status of owning them. As those with capital chose portraits as a way of signifying their status, art moved beyond the monasteries, churches, and castles. Various kinds of images and artwork became a form of social currency, something that advanced in the following centuries down to our own day. However, a key difference to emerge today is the ready access to the trappings of style which Ewen calls the "iconography of prestige," due in large part to the capacity for the cheap reproduction of this iconography.[19]

As signs of status became cheaply available, a new kind of democracy developed, a consumer democracy, wherein most people had access to the styles once reserved for the elites. If not actual wealth, then "the coded look of wealth" came within the means of many. Now machine-cut bric-a-brac glass could give the illusion of hand-cut fine glass. Factories developed processes of embossing and applying veneer that gave their products the look of quality. One commentator named these developments as the "delight in the unreal." Eventually architecture adopted the separation of surface and substance in the way buildings were designed. The development of photography gave everyone except the very poorest access to cheap images. According to Ewen, of all the nineteenth-century developments, photography augmented the power of image over substance as a hallmark of modern style. "Photography became — almost immediately — a prime medium of pretension."[20] Photo studios could invest near-paupers with the accouterments of wealth and status, which they could then proudly display to others.

For several reasons I find Ewen's critique helpful, particularly his historical sense. For the recent trends Goldsmith and Fraser describe with alarming precision, Ewen is able to provide a historical grounding, thanks to his exploration of various points in their origins. Also, his categories, like "style," are worked out so as to provide a coherent and nuanced way of naming cultural phenomena. Finally, his work is filled with detailed examples of current visuals, commercials, and images showing us how they work and helping us learn to think about and analyze such images. At this point I have surveyed four critiques (Baudrillard, Goldsmith, Fraser, Ewen) of a phenomenon in culture variously called simulation, illusion, fashion, style. The critiques of Baudrillard and Ewen, especially for their account of the origins of the phenomenon, are the most complete. One critique, Baudrillard's, seems to say nothing can be done; two, Fraser's and Goldsmith's, do not raise the question of agency. Only one, Ewen's, offers practical, though unsystematized, skills for helping expose the illusions of style. Three of these critiques are in one way or another not fully satisfying. However, together they provide mutually reinforcing points of view that empower us to pay attention to a subtle cultural reality and to learn the analytic skills needed to show how this reality works. Perhaps the complexity of culture is such that it be best approached through a variety of perspectives. There is no single avenue to empowerment on this issue.

## Raymond Williams's Description of Hegemony

In a famous essay written in 1973,[21] Raymond Williams described in detail how people in cultures come to live a kind
of social "totality" which envelops them without their own
awareness. Referring to a widely known essay of the Italian thinker Antonio Gramsci, Williams names this embracing
of a totality "hegemony." For both Gramsci and Williams,
hegemony is a process by which the consent of the dominated classes is obtained for programs not in their best
interests. The dominant classes shape the issues in such a
way that these issues seem to embrace the needs and interests of the subordinate groups at the same time that they
mask and hide the deeper, controlling, and directing interests
of the dominant. Hegemony, then, is not raw overt coer-
cion; it is one group's covert orchestration of compliance by
another group through structuring the consciousness of the
second group. For those who insist on ignoring the significance of class structures and the "interests" behind them,
hegemony is irreversible. Because it shapes consciousness and
action, religious persons need to understand how it works,
and Williams's essay offers a helpful description of these
workings.

Williams explains that hegemony emerges from a total
way of looking at reality that saturates society to such an
extent that it becomes, for those immersed in it, simple common sense. Perhaps a useful current example of hegemony
is the network of common sense, accepted "truths" that
emerge from an economic order of consumption. Persons
are defined as consumers, and readily accept that definition as an appropriate *self-definition* which, as it is lived
out, takes on an even more stubborn taken-for-grantedness.
Hegemony affects consciousness because it affects the patterns of life-practice that shape a life structure. In Williams's
own words:

> [Hegemony] is the central, effective and dominant sys-
> tem of meanings and values, which are not merely

abstract but which are organized and lived. That is why hegemony is not to be understood at the level of mere opinion or mere manipulation. It is a whole body of practices and expectations; our assignments of energy, our ordinary understanding of the nature of man [*sic*] and of his world. It is a set of meanings and values which as [because] they are experienced as practices appear as reciprocally confirming. It thus constitutes a sense of reality for most people in the society, a sense of absolute, because experienced, reality beyond which it is very difficult for most members of the society to move, in most areas of their lives.[22]

If hegemony is more than consciousness but an entire "way" of being in the world, it is not a static system but is actively being reproduced in the rising generations, especially by what Williams calls "the systems of incorporation into a society." Finding "great social significance" in these modes of incorporation, he cites educational institutions and the wide social training found in families as key agencies for the transmission of hegemony.[23]

Not only is hegemony an active process in the sense it is lived; it is also highly adaptive, ever ready to co-opt even critiques within its wider definitions of reality. Thus it can embrace alternative visions, opinions, meanings, and values, accommodating and tolerating them within the dominant culture, but never allowing them to go beyond the limits of the central controlling definitions. The example Williams uses here is parliamentary democracy, which tolerates opposing parties with real oppositions between them, but always within certain pre-set unquestioned limits.[24]

Williams's description of hegemony is so laid out that he at first seems to be saying there is no hope of countering it. Yet Williams's life-work was to point out the stubborn-because-unseen structures that tend to determine our lives so they can be contested and then shifted. As a cultural critic, he brings out of hiding procedures and processes that have a human face and a human form, which he then "photographs

and fingerprints." Giles Gunn suggests that the very introduction of the concept of hegemony into the study of culture
is liberative, since it compels "students of culture to raise
new questions about what might be called its politics of organization," and thus approach their study with heightened
suspicion.[25]

In the above quote from Williams's essay, the last sentence
contains his own conviction about countering hegemony:
"It thus constitutes a sense of reality...beyond which it is
very difficult for most members of the society to move...."
The key words here are "very difficult for most members,"
because if their significance is not held on to, the reader
might conclude no opposition to hegemony is possible. But
Williams's critique is not toward such powerlessness. After
the cited passage, he goes on to remind us that human reality is so complex that it cannot be entirely contained within
these boundaries. "No dominant culture in reality exhausts
the full range of human practice, human energy, human
intention...."[26] There are always residual elements, experiences, meanings, and values, which hang on, seemingly out
of place in the dominant culture, but still possessing at least
a latent power to question the hegemonic system. The reason they survive is that they cannot be expressed in terms
of the dominant culture or are not taken seriously by it, and
so they continue to be lived and practiced. The first example
Williams gives of such residual elements are religious values
that have somehow escaped being sucked into the hegemonic
pattern.

In addition to residual elements carried on from an earlier period, Williams cites "emergent elements" as also able
to function outside the hegemony. These are "new meanings
and values, new practices, new significance and experiences"
that are continually being created. However, since the dominant culture is on the alert for these emergent elements so
as to incorporate them, they are not likely to be overlooked
as insignificant the way residual elements are. If anything,
the speed of communications allows hegemonic controls to
be quickly extended over such new developments. Still, these

emergent elements can be lived as alternatives to the dominant system or in actual opposition to it, acting as an agent of change.

One could say that any marginal class pushed to the fringes of society especially by economic pressures could come to represent values and practices outside the hegemonic system. The same might be true of religious groups, practicing the ultimate meanings and vision of their own scriptures. If their religious stance caused them to embrace the plight of the marginalized, they might represent a potential challenge to the dominant culture. At least they could provide a wedge in the seemingly impenetrable facade of hegemony. Similarly the young, who seem so inexorably and easily brought under the hegemonic "umbrella," could ironically have within them a sense of emerging patterns of an alternate practice.[27] That the young are quick to adopt the trappings of the dominant system should not blind us to the possibility they may harbor within themselves intimations of radical alternatives or may be more ready than others to examine the contradictions latent in any social system. Whatever the power and subtle effectiveness of hegemony, then, Williams reminds us of its incompleteness in the face of human questioning and creativity. Such reminders are liberating.

Paul Willis and Philip Corrigan also remind us that often in the very things that cannot be spoken by the young can be found clues to how they may be resisting the dominant hegemony. Speaking specifically about working class youth, they hold that "the *texture* of working class cultural forms needs...careful decoding" so as to disclose the ways these youths seek to limit and counter the oppression they have experienced.[28] Though in my view the examples they cite offer only marginal resistance to the dominant culture, they do show how any culture, as a human creation, has within it at least latent possibilities of questioning, countering, if not actual reversal. The ties that people have to one another offer the possibilities that they may respond to the injustices suffered by their fellows. These ties also offer opportunities to mock the hegemonic system as a way of recognizing the contradictions in it and of resisting it.[29]

A fine explanation of how such a break in a hegemonic system might take place is given us by Gregory Baum. He points out how every society has dominant classes and authoritative institutions which produce a culture to support their own power. Within such societies, however, are strata without access to the power or privileges of the elites. The same society viewed by these marginals is quite different from that viewed by the privileged. What the marginals live contradicts what the privileged claim. This contradiction is not just a verbal one; it is societal, embedded in the social structures themselves. However much overlooked or even disguised by those in power, this contradiction can, at any time, become the source of various kinds of protest actions on the part of the underclass. The version of reality fostered by the privileged can become brittle before the actuality of the marginals. As Baum puts it:

> From the lower strata become visible the weaknesses, injustices and contradictions that remain hidden from those identified with the dominant structures. The modes of thought accepted by a culture and the social virtues recommended by it have an ugly underside that is discoverable by the inferiorized groups. People of the lower strata express their protest against the world that oppresses them in religious or secular symbols of various kinds, and when they gain access to learning they are able to develop modes of thought and advocate values that transcend the dominant culture.[30]

This last point of Baum's is particularly important for an understanding of cultural agency. The marginalized may create their own versions of reality that transcend the dominant culture and by doing so, relativize it. Such an ability to think outside of or beyond the assumptions of the dominant culture takes root in a new imagination of how society might be. Such imaginations are not usually found in the centers of power. Instead they "usually emerge in marginal movements, like the movement started by Jesus of Nazareth, that are repudiated by the defenders of the dominant structures and survive only by remaining partially underground."

Along with Williams, Willis, and Corrigan, Baum encourages us to note the contradictions present in any society, to find out how these affect various groups within society, and to work with them to explore both the contradictions and alternative visions and practices.[31] Many people have an intuitive sense of these contradictions which they perhaps have not yet named, but which they are ready to consider if brought to their attention in the right way. As Baum says, "Popular leaders are required...who are able to put into words the frustrations which people suffer and provide a new imagination."[32] For example, young people, initially unable to name the violence inflicting pain and disruption in their lives, can come to recognize and name it, and, further, to find ways of countering it. Skill in naming these contradictions does not require a university degree.

A study further supporting Williams's position that hegemony cannot embrace all of social practice is Eugene Genovese's *Roll, Jordan, Roll,* a study of the culture of U.S. slaves.[33] Genovese's book shows how religion can become — and in the situations of slave oppression did become — a force for disrupting hegemony. While never downplaying the oppression and exploitation of slavery, Genovese points out that human beings do not consent to being only victims. They work to construct a human life, creating their own sources of joy and hope. Because their masters needed something from slaves — their work — in the end they had to compromise to a certain extent with the slaves' own resistance to dehumanization.[34] Thus, at the corn-husking festivals, the slaves were able to make of overtime work a festival of sorts, whose work songs were examples of improvised social criticism.

At some level, the religion lived by the slaves had within it a powerful alternative vision of human dignity, showing up the oppression for what it was. In its preaching of the dignity and worth of all persons, Christianity, even in its Pauline exhortations to submission, sowed the seeds of defiance of authority. As Genovese puts it, the doctrine: Render unto Caesar the things that are Caesar's and unto God the things that are God's, "is deceptively two-edged. If it calls for political submission to the powers that be, it also calls for militant defense of the freedom of the spirit and the autonomy of the personality."[35] The religious vision embraced by the Afro-American slaves by no means called for full docility and submission. On the lips of the black preachers especially, the biblical message "proclaimed the freedom and inviolability of the human soul."[36] Eventually that call triumphed.

## The Capacity for Cultural Transcendence: Criticism of Culture

In the last section I cited Gregory Baum's description of how those living on the underside of culture can come to name its contradictions ignored by the dominant classes. Baum uses the expression "cultural transcendence" for this process of ceasing to take culture for granted. Giles Gunn's book, *The Culture of Criticism and the Criticism of Culture,* explores the quest for cultural transcendence in the United States and in our own century. Gunn examines the principal literary and cultural critics after 1950, finding that literary critics have consistently raised such questions about culture that their work would have to be now ranked under cultural criticism. This critique of culture was relatively new, as Gunn suggests in a survey of Rene Welleck's six-volume *History of Modern Criticism,* where the word "culture" does not occur until the fourth volume. The omission does not mean that culture was not dealt with, only that the way culture was conceived of did not allow it to be named. Gunn points out that every theory of literary criticism is implicitly a theory of culture. He holds that the critical stance is not just a product of modern culture but one of its most characteristic practices, so much that "to comprehend *culture* in its relationship to *criticism* is to fathom at least one dimension of the meaning of the word *modern*."[37] Gunn, then, clearly implies that cultural transcendence is both a characteristic and consequence of all modern critical thought.

Although searching for cultural transcendence, this kind of thought does not operate under the aegis of religious transcendence, not because it has no ethical or moral underpinnings or even because it is insensitive to the sacred. It, rather, is suspicious of the very "habits of mind" that were historically preoccupied with metaphysical or ontological ultimacy. The actual suspicion is that these habits of mind, and the institutions within which they operated, functioned as "subterfuges for the expression of various kinds of social, cultural, political, and even religious privilege" and have thus lost their credibility with many Western intellectuals.[38] And so this disbelief, as more a kind of skepticism of motives than religious doubt, has led to creative avenues of intellectual inquiry that make possible further and more discriminating thought.

Lionel Trilling, to whose thought Gunn devotes considerable attention, expressed the overall cast of mind of modern cultural criticism when he stated his own goal as

> to see literary situations as cultural situations and cultural situations as great elaborate fights about moral issues, and moral issues as having something to do with gratuitously chosen images of personal being.[39]

Gunn believes that were one to change "literary situations" into "religious" or "political" or "social" or "cultural" or "intellectual situations," one would have a good description of books of cultural criticism by persons like Niebuhr, Lippmann, Riesmann, Rieff, or Hofstadter, respectively. Throughout his book, Gunn shows how the "mode of discourse" in which moral concerns have been kept alive in modern U.S. culture is that of cultural criticism.

Concerned as I have been with finding ways of becoming active in seeing "how we see" in a time of electronic communications, I find Gunn's survey encouraging. He reminds me of developments among intellectuals that I had not connected with my own work and shows how these persons increasingly have come to look at the relationship between a social order and the signifying system that shapes the spirits of those living in it. As Gunn implies toward the end of his book, their critiques are becoming more and more astute at discerning the interconnectedness of thought and social structure.[40] Underlying the deep moral concern of these persons is a radical humanism that believes the human vocation involves encompassing one's actual biological, psychological, economic, social, or historical circumstances by means of comprehension:

> In saying "No" to all that limits or restricts, they [these humanist critics] have implicitly maintained, we say "Yes" to the spiritual freedom that permits us to imagine otherwise. Hence the centrality in their humanism of the experience of art itself, whose moral function is for them identical with its imaginative function: to express the measure of our independence from those very systems of meaning we have created in culture — indeed, *as* culture — to define and enact ourselves.[41]

These critics then assume that human beings can transcend the meanings by which they have defined themselves. Though no one can live outside culture, persons can achieve standpoints different from culture's hegemonic versions of what the meaning of their lives should be. Another way of putting this point is that *the noblest or most significant expressions of any culture are those that contain the culture's most searching assessment of itself.* In my view religious sensibility leads to just such assessment.

## Another Look at the Religious Question

At this point I wish to return to the questions with which I began this chapter, which, in fact, are not so different from the questions underlying this book as a whole. What are the possibilities of cultural analysis? Is the power of those shaping consciousness through electronic communications so great that we delude ourselves if we suppose we can counter it? And, of course, could it be that a particular approach to cultural analysis would, in the end, tend to discourage rather than encourage efforts to introduce many others to the skills of such analysis?

If I take the last question first, my answer is no: any accurate description, to a certain extent even a totalizing one, could be helpful. It could lead to action if only from a kind of quasi-despair. Baudrillard's critique, for all its seeming this-is-the-way-things-are-and-will-be tone, shows me this in my own reaction, which is one of alarm, of telling myself the situation is more serious than I had recognized. Baudrillard, in the end, calls us to action, which I presume is his intent and the reason his writings have been translated into other languages. Similarly, Fraser's and Goldsmith's descriptions-without-prescriptions of contemporary mores call, in their own way, for greater attention to overlooked trends.

If Williams's account of hegemony at first makes it seem like a closed hatch sealing us in, he eventually opens us to an understanding of the ways that persons inevitably contest culture. All human beings naturally contest oppression when they come to see it; the process of coming to see it lays the foundation of contestation. Questioning and contestation seem to be built into the vocation of human beings. As a working hypothesis, such an assumption itself calls for the liberating work of cultural analysis.

I believe that religious persons have the potential for a critique of culture as an almost natural outcome of their religious commitment. One could counter, if not scoff at, such a claim by pointing to the many historical examples of the cultural captivity or even enslavement of the religious imagination. Indeed, the conditions under which such captivity has taken place or been avoided deserve a detailed examination not possible here. Gregory Baum suggests a possible clue to the workings of religious cultural contestation in his explanation of how the marginalized come to embrace values transcending the dominant culture. A similar process of transcendence can work in religious groups. As I have pointed out in earlier chapters, religions propose networks of meanings laden with transcendence and ultimacy. Such networks relativize — or at least have a potential to do so — the positions of society and culture. Especially when religious conviction brings communities to embrace the concerns of the marginalized, religious conviction merges with social critique.

To put the matter another way, a religion bears within it resources of hope, based on its religious vision.[42] The religious imagination comprises an alternative vision of life as a reality "hoped for" and worked for in the light of that hope. Such an imagination means that in spite of desperate and long-standing injustice and oppression, in the face of death itself, religious people can harbor an alternative understanding deeply contesting inhuman social structures, including religious structures themselves. This alternative understanding does not wait impassively for change but works actively at the most subversive of activities: keeping alive a memory of an alternative way of living. From this angle there persists an alternative social possibility, meant by God to become an actuality. Its becoming an actuality is basically a work of God, a holy task in which persons carry forward God's will. From a religious point of view, one's religious vocation calls for one to protest and contest what is inhuman — even when one judges little might be accomplished. No wonder those wanting to keep a social system unquestioned and unchanged find the religious imagination "dangerous." Indeed, one would have to admit it represents a volatile social force that, in certain circumstances, could be a potent force for evil.[43] In commenting on the emergence of the current "culture of criticism," Giles Gunn points to both the "problem and possibility" of religion, writing:

> [T]he category of religion is no mere superfluity in current critical controversy but one of its principal enablers and chief elements.... There is an obsession with the problem and possibility to which religion attests: the existence of modalities of experience that remain ultimately unconditioned by what is now called either

the privileges of perception or the predispositions of power.[44]

In our day, more and more religious persons are becoming alarmed at the power of electronic media to shape the imagination of the meaning of life. Some propose solutions that would impose tight religious social controls.[45] In my view, the religious task in a situation of pluralism involves no master plan of social control, seeking to impose its own vision on all. Instead, the task is that of living the religious vision with integrity, and through the mimetic power of that way of life, to invite others to share that vision. In a pluralist situation, again, religious communities would have to find allies, religious or not, willing to challenge the society to become economically and politically a more human social order.

I doubt the particular problems of encouraging the kind of agency involved in cultural analysis can ever be resolved in a final, formulaic pattern, free of conflict. The ongoing process of questioning culture while affirming all that is positive in it is bound to be conflictual, but in a creative sense, calling for the re-examination of basic assumptions and of actual ways of living. This book was written out of the conviction that engaging in that process is part of the human, and religious, vocation.

# NOTES

1. Gregory Baum presents George Grant's *Technology and Justice* as an example of describing a situation in a way that increases powerlessness. Baum names Grant's problem as a "totalizing" critique. I would think that even in works not "totalizing" there can be ways of approaching situations that inhibit action and foster a sense of powerlessness. See Gregory Baum, "Technology and Enlightenment," *The Ecumenist* 27, no. 5 (July–August 1989): 75–77. Baum writes:

> I call a social theory "totalizing" when it offers a world interpretation in accordance with a single paradigm. One paradigm is here thought to explain the course of an entire historical period. Totalizing theories are inevitably deterministic. When totalizing theories are offered out of a position of power, they are called ideologies. George

Grant's totalizing interpretation of technological society is offered out of a position of complete powerlessness. We cannot change the orientation of modern society because every such effort will itself be subverted by the logic of technology and make things worse rather than better. In my opinion, George Grant's theory increases our powerlessness.

2. Clifford Geertz, *The Interpretation of Cultures* (New York: Harper Colophon Books, 1973), pp. 33–34.

3. For a scathing attack on inept action as a way of avoiding the true scope of a problem, see Kirkpatrick Sale, "The Trouble with Earth Day," *The Nation* (30 April 1990): 594–98.

4. Mark Poster, ed., *Jean Baudrillard: Selected Writings* (Stanford, Calif.: Stanford University Press, 1988), p. 5. Poster finds Baudrillard's totalizing tendencies a flaw.

5. Ibid., pp. 166–67.

6. Ibid., pp. 167–68.

7. Ibid., p. 172.

8. Ibid., pp. 172–74. Even his compatriot Bourdieu's insight that "the specific character of every relation of force is to dissimulate itself, thus acquiring all its force because it is dissimulated" cannot be successfully applied to capital because the very denunciation in the insight misunderstands the role of symbolic violence as a kind of *violence beyond force*. Indeed, Baudrillard seems to ridicule Bourdieu here.

9. Doug Kellner, "Postmodernism as Social Theory," *Theory, Culture, and Society* 5 (1988): 239–69, at 245. I have found Kellner's summary of Baudrillard's positions very helpful.

10. "The Masses: The Implosion of the Social in the Media," in *Selected Writings*, pp. 207–19. At the end of this essay, Baudrillard does offer a hypothesis that hidden in the abdication of the masses is a kind of resistance, but I found his argument cryptic.

11. Barbara Goldsmith, "The Meaning of Celebrity," *New York Times Magazine* (4 December 1983): 75ff., at 75.

12. Ibid., 76.

13. Kennedy Fraser, *The Fashionable Mind* (Boston: David R. Godine, 1985), pp. 145–59. The title essay, placed symbolically at the very center of her book, first appeared in the *New Yorker* (13 March 1978). Citations in this paragraph are from pp. 145–46.

14. Ibid., p. 148. Note the similarity of Fraser's ideas with these comments of Baudrillard about fashion's relation to simulation models:

> Just as the model is more real than the real . . . , acquiring thus a vertiginous impression of truth, the amazing aspect of fashion is that it is more beautiful than the beautiful: it is fascinating. Its seductive ca-

pacity is independent of all judgments. It exceeds the aesthetic form
in the ecstatic form of unconditional metamorphosis.

Whereas the aesthetic form always implies a moral distinction between the beautiful and the ugly, the estatic form is immoral. If there
is a secret to fashion, beyond the sheer pleasures of art and taste, it
is this immorality, the sovereignty of ephemeral models. (*Selected
Writings*, p. 186)

15. Stuart Ewen, *All-Consuming Images: The Politics of Style in Contemporary Culture* (New York: Basic Books, 1988).

16. Ibid., p. 14.

17. Ibid., pp. 19–20.

18. Ibid., p. 23.

19. Ibid., pp. 26–30. Although Ewen does not mention Baudrillard's
work, his historical survey supports Baudrillard's overview of the phases
of simulation. See *Selected Writings*, pp. 166–84, and Kellner, "Postmodernism," pp. 244–45. Background for Ewen's historical survey includes Lester Little, *Religious Poverty and the Profit Economy in Medieval
Europe* (Ithaca, N.Y.: Cornell University Press, 1978), chapters 1 and 2.

20. Ewen, *All-Consuming Images*, p. 39.

21. Raymond Williams, "Base and Superstructure in Marxist Cultural
Theory," in *Problems in Materialism and Culture* (New York: Schocken
Books, 1980), pp. 31–49. Also in Roger Dale et al., *Schooling and Capitalism: A Sociological Reader* (London: Routledge and Kegan Paul, 1976),
pp. 202–10.

22. Williams, "Base," p. 38.

23. Some Marxist critiques of educational structures provide valuable
material on hegemony, which is reinforced by schooling structures. For
an overview, see Henry Giroux, "Theories of Reproduction and Resistance in the New Sociology of Education: A Critical Analysis," *Harvard
Educational Review* 53, no. 3 (August 1983): 257–93.

24. Williams, "Base," pp. 39–40.

25. Giles Gunn, *The Culture of Criticism and the Criticism of Culture*
(New York: Oxford University Press, 1987), p. 166.

26. Williams, "Base," p. 43. Below I am following pp. 40–45.

27. Readers with special interest in this question would find helpful Karl Mannheim, "The Problem of Generations," in *Essays on the
Sociology of Knowledge* (London: Routledge and Kegan Paul, 1972).

28. Paul Willis and Philip Corrigan, "Orders of Experience: The Differences of Working Class Cultural Forms," *Social Text* 7 (1983): 85–103, at
100–101. Michel Foucault writes in a similar vein about "subjugated and
disqualified knowledges" found among local and popular groups. Though
often overlooked by mainstream scholarship, these "knowledges" deserve
scholarly attention. See Michel Foucault, "Two Lectures," in Colin Gor-

don, ed., *Michel Foucault: Power/Knowledge — Selected Interviews and Writings* (New York: Pantheon, 1980), pp. 78–108.

29. Willis and Corrigan, "Orders," p. 102. These ideas are from an essay by G. M. Sider, cited by Willis and Corrigan.

30. Gregory Baum, *Truth beyond Relativism: Karl Mannheim's Sociology of Knowledge* (Milwaukee: Marquette University Press, 1977), p. 61, here and below. This book is the text of a lecture and is brief, but important.

31. For a corroborating view of the kinds of contradiction built into economic systems, see Ernest Mandel, *Late Capitalism* (New York: Schocken Verso Books, 1978), and *Long Waves of Capitalist Development: The Marxist Interpretation* (London: Cambridge University Press, 1980), p. 115.

32. Baum, *Truth*, p. 62

33. Eugene D. Genovese, *Roll, Jordan, Roll: The World the Slaves Made* (New York: Pantheon Books, 1974). I am grateful to Brian Lynch for making me aware of Genovese's interest in counter-hegemony.

34. Ibid., p. 317. Of course oppressors are skilled at allowing their victims just enough "happiness" to foster docility. Genovese seems alert to the complexities of this matter. Genovese's insights here would not apply to the Nazi death camps, where the goal was death and work was a system geared toward death, though even some of the Holocaust literature shows how the human spirit was able to triumph in the face of death.

35. Ibid., p. 165.

36. Ibid., pp. 166–67.

37. Gunn, *Culture of Criticism*, p. 5.

38. Ibid., p. x.

39. Ibid., p. xi.

40. See especially ibid., chapter 7, "American Studies as Cultural Criticism."

41. Ibid., p. 26, here and below.

42. I use this expression after reflecting on Raymond Williams's posthumously collected essays: *Resources of Hope* (London and New York: Verso Books, 1989).

43. A body of religious thought espouses non-violence as a fundamental way of avoiding such evil. A thought-provoking analysis of the religious bases of violent social conflict *and* of its opposite, cohesive social pluralism, is Aloysius Pieris, "Faith-Communities and Communalism," *East Asian Pastoral Review* 26, nos. 3–4 (1989): 294–310.

44. Gunn, *Culture of Criticism*, p. 176.

45. For an examination of a proposal for dealing with the "two cultures," the religious and secular, see William L. Sachs, "Willimon's Project: Does It Make Sense?" *The Christian Century* 106, no. 13 (19 April 1989): 412–14. Sachs's questions illustrate the complexity of the issues once a concrete proposal is made.

# BIBLIOGRAPHY

Adelson, Andrea. "Study Attacks Women's Roles in TV." *New York Times* (19 November 1990): L18.

Apple, Michael. "The Hidden Curriculum and the Nature of Conflict." In William J. Pinar, ed., *Curriculum Theorizing: The Reconceptualists.* Berkeley, Calif.: McCutcheon, 1975.

———. *Ideology and Curriculum.* Boston: Routledge and Kegan Paul, 1979.

———. "Reproduction, Contestation, and Curriculum: An Essay in Self-Criticism." *Interchange* 12, nos. 2–3 (1981): 27–47.

———. *Education and Power.* Boston: Routledge and Kegan Paul, 1982.

———. "Class, Culture and the State in Educational Interventions." In Robert Everhard, ed., *The Predominant Orthodoxy.* New York: Ballinger Press, 1983.

———. "Work, Gender, and Teaching." *Teachers College Record* 84, no. 3 (1983): 611–28.

Apple, Michael, and Thomas Brady. "Toward Increasing the Potency of Student Rights Claims: Advocacy-Oriented Policy Recommendations." In V. Hanbrich and M. Apple, eds., *Schooling and the Rights of Children.* Berkeley, Calif.: McCutcheon, 1975.

———. "Analyzing Determinations: Understanding and Evaluating the Production of Social Outcomes in Schools." *Curriculum Inquiry* 10, no. 1 (1980): 55–76.

Archer, Chris. *Biting the Bullet: Personal Reflections on Religious Education.* Edinburgh: St. Andrew Press, 1990.

———, ed. *Religion and the Media: An Introductory Reader.* Cardiff: University of Wales Press, 1993.

Aronowitz, Stanley, and Henry Giroux. "Mass Culture and Critical Pedagogy." *Education under Siege.* Granby, Mass.: Bergin and Garvey, 1985.

Atlas, James. "Beyond Demographics." *Atlantic Monthly* (October 1984): 49–58.

Bagdikian, Ben H. "The Lords of the Global Village." *The Nation* (12 June 1989): 805–20.

Barnet, Richard. "Reflections: Rethinking National Strategy." *New Yorker* (21 March 1988): 104–14.

————, and John Cavanagh. *Global Dreams: Imperial Corporations and the New World Order.* New York: Simon and Schuster, 1994.

Baum, Gregory. *Truth beyond Relativism: Karl Mannheim's Sociology of Knowledge.* Milwaukee: Marquette University Press, 1977.

————. "Faith and Culture." *The Ecumenist* 24, no. 1 (November–December 1985): 9–13.

————. "The Labor Pope in Canada." *The Ecumenist* 23, no. 2 (January–February 1985): 17–23.

————. "Option for the Powerless." *The Ecumenist* 26, no. 1 (November–December 1987): 5–11.

————. "Technology and Enlightenment." *The Ecumenist* 27, no. 5 (July–August 1989): 75–77.

Beirne, Charles J. "Jesuit Education for Justice: The Colegio in El Salvador, 1968–84." *Harvard Educational Review* 55, no. 1 (1985): 1–19.

Bell, Brenda, John Gaventa, and John Peters, eds. *We Make the Road by Walking: Myles Horton and Paulo Freire: Conversations on Education and Social Change.* Philadelphia: Temple University Press, 1990.

Bellah, Robert N., et al. *Habits of the Heart: Individualism and Commitment in American Life.* Berkeley: University of California Press, 1985.

Benjamin, Walter. "The Work of Art in the Age of Mechanical Reproduction." In Hannah Arendt, ed., *Illuminations.* New York: Harcourt, Brace, 1968.

Bloom, Allan. *The Closing of the American Mind.* New York: Simon and Schuster, 1987.

Boff, Leonardo. "Theological Characteristics of a Grassroots Church." In S. Torres and J. Eagleson, eds., *The Challenge of Basic Christian Communities.* Maryknoll, N.Y.: Orbis, 1981.

Borgmann, Albert. *Crossing the Postmodern Divide.* Chicago: University of Chicago Press, 1993.

Bourdieu, Pierre. *Outline of Theory and Practice.* Cambridge: Cambridge University Press, 1977.

————. *Distinction: A Social Critique of the Judgment of Taste.* Cambridge, Mass.: Harvard University Press, 1984.

Boyer, Peter J. "Toy-Based TV: Effects on Children Debates." *New York Times* (3 February 1986): A1ff.

Braga, Maria Lucia Santaella. "For a Classification of Visual Signs." *Semiotica* 70, nos. 1/2 (1988): 59–78.

Carlsson-Paige, Nancy, and Diane E. Levin. *Who's Calling the Shots? How to Respond Effectively to Children's Fascination with War Play and War Toys.* Philadelphia: New Society Publishers, 1990.

Collins, Glenn. "Controversy about Toys, TV Violence." *New York Times* (12 December 1985): C1.

Crawford, Marisa, and Graham Rossiter. *Missionaries to a Teenage Culture: Religious Education in a Time of Rapid Change.* Sydney: Christian Brothers Resource Group, 1988.

Dale, Roger. *Schooling and Capitalism: A Sociological Reader.* London: Routledge and Kegan Paul, 1976.

D'Amboise, Jacques. "I Show a Child What Is Possible." *Boston Sunday Globe Parade* (6 August 1989): 6.

Davis, Charles. "Religion and the Sense of the Sacred." Catholic Theological Society of America, *Proceedings* 31 (1976): 87–105.

Denby, David. "Buried Alive: Our Children and the Avalanche of Crud." *New Yorker* (15 July 1996): 48–58.

Dougherty, Philip H. "Advertising: Inside Children's Television." *New York Times* (20 May 1987): D19.

Ewen, Stuart. *All-Consuming Images: The Politics of Style in Contemporary Culture.* New York: Basic Books, 1988.

Farley, Edward. *Ecclesial Reflection: An Anatomy of Theological Method.* Philadelphia: Fortress Press, 1982.

Fasching, D. J. "Theologian of Culture." *Cross Currents* 35, no. 1 (1985): 9–10.

Fitzgerald, Frances. "Onwards and Upwards with the Arts: History Textbooks." *New Yorker,* 26 February, 5 March, and 12 March 1979.

Fore, William F. "Analyzing the Military-News Complex." *The Christian Century* (17 April 1991): 422–23.

Foucault, Michel. "Two Lectures." In Colin Gordon, ed., *Michel Foucault: Power/Knowledge — Selected Interviews and Writings.* New York: Pantheon, 1980.

Fraser, Kennedy. *The Fashionable Mind.* Boston: David R. Godine, 1985.

Freire, Paulo. *Cultural Action for Freedom.* Cambridge, Mass.: Harvard Educational Review and the Center for the Study of Development and Social Change, Monograph Series no. 1, 1970.

———. *Education for Critical Consciousness.* New York: Seabury Press, 1973.

———. *The Politics of Education.* Granby, Mass.: Bergin and Garvey, 1985.

Fussell, Paul. *Wartime: Understanding and Behavior in the Second World War.* New York: Oxford University Press, 1989.

Gates, Henry Louis, Jr. "Whose Canon Is It Anyway?" *New York Times Book Review* (26 February 1989): 1, 44–45.

Gebauer, Gunter, and Christoph Wulf. *Mimesis: Culture, Art, Society.* Trans. Don Reneau. Berkeley: University of California Press, 1995.

Geertz, Clifford. "Religion as a Cultural System," and "Ethos, World View, and the Analysis of Sacred Symbols." In *The Interpretation of Cultures.* New York: Basic Books, 1973.

Genovese, Eugene D. *Roll, Jordon, Roll: The World the Slaves Made.* New York: Pantheon Books, 1974.

Gerbner, George. "The Challenge of Television." Unpublished paper, Annenberg School of Communication, University of Pennsylvania.

Giddens, Anthony. *Central Problems in Social Theory: Action, Structure, and Contradiction in Social Analysis.* Berkeley: University of California Press, 1979.

Giroux, Henry A. "Theories of Reproduction and Resistance in the New Sociology of Education: A Critical Analysis." *Harvard Educational Review* 53, no. 3 (1985): 257–93.

———. "Consuming Social Change: The 'United Colors of Benetton.'" *Cultural Critique* 26 (1993–94): 5–32.

Goffman, Erving. *Gender Advertisements.* New York: Harper Colophon Books, 1979.

Goldman, Ari L. "Religion Notes." *New York Times* (30 November 1986): 66.

Goldsmith, Barbara. "The Meaning of Celebrity." *New York Times Magazine* (4 December 1983): 75ff.

Gombrich, E. H. *Art and Illusion: A Study in the Psychology of Pictorial Representation.* New York: Pantheon Books, 1960.

Gopnik, Adam. "A Critic at Large: Read All about It." *New Yorker* (12 December 1994): 84–102.

Greeley, Andrew. *A Theology of Popular Culture.* Chicago: Thomas More, 1988.

Gunn, Giles. *The Culture of Criticism and the Criticism of Culture.* New York: Oxford University Press, 1987.

Gutiérrez, Gustavo. *We Drink from Our Own Wells.* Maryknoll, N.Y.: Orbis Books, 1984.

Hartshorne, Charles, and Paul Weiss, eds. *Collected Papers of Charles Sanders Peirce,* vols. 1 and 2. Cambridge, Mass.: The Belknap Press of Harvard University Press, 1965.

Hechinger, Fred M. "About Education: TV's Pitch to Children." *New York Times* (17 March 1987): C9.

Higgins, M. D. "The Tyranny of Images: Aspects of Hidden Control... Literature, Ethnography, and Political Commentary in the West of Ireland." *The Crane Bag* (Dublin) 8, no. 2 (1984): 132–42.

Holland, Joe. "Linking Social Analysis and Theological Reflection: The Place of Root Metaphors in Social and Religious Experience." In James E. Hug, ed., *Tracing the Spirit.* New York: Paulist Press, 1983.

Huizinga, John. "Patriotism and Nationalism in European History." In *Men and Ideas.* New York: Meridian Books, 1959.

Inglis, Fred. *Raymond Williams.* New York: Routledge, 1995.

John Paul II. "Children and the Media." *Origins* 9, no. 3 (7 June 1979): 33–47.

———. "Meeting with Catholic Educators September 1984 St. John the Baptist Basilica, St. John's Newfoundland." *Canadian Catholic Review* (October 1984): 346–47.

―――. *Christifideles Laici: On the Vocation and the Mission of the Lay Faithful in the Church and in the World.* Vatican City: Libreria Editrice Vaticana, 1988.

Johnson, Kirk. "Schools Test the Environmental Waters." *New York Times* (21 November 1989): B1, B6.

Jungmann, Josef. "Religious Education in Late Medieval Times." In Gerard S. Sloyan, ed., *Shaping the Christian Message.* New York: Macmillan, 1958.

Kavanaugh, John. "Capitalist Culture as a Religious and Educational Formation System." *Religious Education* 78, no. 1 (Winter 1983): 50–60.

―――. "The World of Wealth and the Gods of Wealth." In L. Boff and V. Elizondo, eds., *Option for the Poor: Challenge to the Rich Countries. Concilium* 187 (1986).

Kellner, Doug. "Postmodernism as Social Theory." *Theory, Culture and Society* 5 (1988): 239–69.

Kennedy, William B., and Everett C. Parker. "On Control: A Discussion of the Ethical and Moral Issues Arising from Current Communication Policies and Practices." *Religious Education* 82, no. 2 (1987): 203–17.

―――. "Understanding Media: An Interview with Robert Liebert." *Religious Education* 82, no. 2 (1987): 191–202.

Kleist, J. A., ed. *The Ancient Christian Writers,* no. 6. New York: Newman Press, 1948.

Kowzan, Tadeusz. "Iconisme ou Mimetisme?" *Semiotica* 71, nos. 3/4 (1988): 213–26.

Kubey, Robert. "A Body at Rest Tends to Remain Glued to the Tube." *New York Times* (5 August 1990): H47.

Lakoff, George, and Mark Johnson. *Metaphors We Live By.* Chicago: University of Chicago Press, 1980.

Lappe, Frances Moore. *What to Do after You Turn Off the TV.* New York: Ballantine, 1985.

Levinson, Daniel. *The Seasons of a Man's Life.* New York: Alfred A. Knopf, 1978.

―――, with Judy D. Levinson. *The Seasons of a Woman's Life.* New York: Knopf, 1996.

Liebert, Robert M., and Joyce Sprafkin. *The Early Window: Effects of Television on Children and Youth.* New York: Pergamon Press, 1988.

Lipovetsky, Gilles. *The Empire of Fashion.* Trans. Catherine Porter. Princeton, N.J.: Princeton University Press, 1994.

Little, Lester. *Religious Poverty and the Profit Economy in Medieval Europe.* Ithaca, N.Y.: Cornell University Press, 1978.

Luhmann, Nicholas. *Love as Passion: The Codification of Intimacy.* Cambridge, Mass.: Harvard University Press, 1986.

MacCabe, Colin. Raymond Williams's obituary in the journal *Z* (April 1988): 59.

MacIntyre, Alisdair. *First Principles, Final Ends, and Contemporary Philosophical Issues*. Milwaukee: Marquette University Press, 1990.

MacKinnon, Catharine A. "Pornography, Civil Rights, and Speech." *Harvard Civil Rights–Civil Liberties Law Review* 20 (1985): 1–70.

———. "Desire and Power: A Feminist Perspective." In Cary Nelson and Lawrence Grossberg, eds., *Marxism and the Interpretation of Culture*. Chicago: University of Chicago Press, 1988.

———. *Only Words*. Cambridge, Mass.: Harvard University Press, 1993.

Macmurray, John. *Persons in Relation*. London: Faber and Faber, 1961.

Mandel, Ernest. *Late Capitalism*. New York: Schocken Verso Books, 1978.

———. *Long Waves of Capitalist Development: The Marxist Interpretation*. London: Cambridge University Press, 1980.

Mannheim, Karl. "The Problem of Generations." In *Essays on the Sociology of Knowledge*. London: Routledge and Kegan Paul, 1972.

Marrou, Henri. *A History of Education in Antiquity*. Trans. George Lamb. Madison: University of Wisconsin Press, 1982.

Marx, Karl, and Friedrich Engels. *The German Ideology*. Cited in Raymond Williams, "Ideology," chapter 4 of *Marxism and Literature*. New York: Oxford University Press, 1977.

Maslin, Janet. "Over the Top." *New York Times* (2 February 1987): C21.

Mattelart, Armand, and Seth Siegelaub. *Communication and Class Struggle*. New York: International General, 1979.

Mayenowa, M. R. "An Analysis of Some Visual Signs: Suggestions for Analysis." In Jan van der Eng and Majmir Grygaer, eds., *The Structure of Texts and the Semiotics of Culture*. The Hague: Mouton, 1973.

Miles, Margaret. "The Recovery of Asceticism." *Commonweal* (28 January 1983): 40–43.

———. *Image as Insight: Visual Understanding in Western Christianity and Secular Culture*. Boston: Beacon Press, 1985.

———. *Practicing Christianity: Critical Perspectives for an Embodied Christianity*. New York: Crossroad, 1988.

Miller, Mark Crispin. *Boxed-In: The Culture of TV*. Evanston, Ill.: Northwestern University Press, 1988.

———. "Hollywood: The Ad." *Atlantic Monthly* (April 1990): 41–68.

Milosz, Czeslaw. *The Witness of Poetry*. Cambridge, Mass.: Harvard University Press, 1983.

Moran, Richard. "Seeing and Believing: Metaphor, Image, and Force." *Critical Inquiry* 16 (Autumn 1989): 87–112.

Mowlana, Hamid. "Mass Media and Culture: Toward an Integrated Theory." In William B. Gudykunst, ed., *Intercultural Communication*

*Theory: Current Perspectives*. Beverly Hills, Calif.: Sage Publications, 1983.

National Coalition on Television Violence. "NCTV Estimate on Impact of Violence." *NCTV News* 8, nos. 3–4 (July–August 1987).

National Council of the Churches of Christ in the USA. *Violence and Sexual Violence in Film, Television, Cable, and Home Video*. Report of a Study Commission of the Communication Commission. New York: Communication Commission, National Council of Churches, 1985.

Ong, Walter. "Literacy and Orality in Our Times." *Journal of Communication* (Winter 1980): 197–204.

Opie, Iona, and Peter Opie. *Children's Games in Street and Playground*. New York: Oxford University Press, 1985.

Orwell, George. "The Sporting Spirit." In *Selected Writings*. London: Heinemann, 1947.

O'Toole, Fintan. "Forked Tongues: The Language of Contemporary Politics." *The Furrow* (Ireland) 45, no. 12 (1994): 675–82.

Pieris, Aloysius. "Christianity and Buddhism in Core-to-Core Dialogue." *Cross Currents* 37, no. 1 (Spring 1987): 47–75.

———. "Faith-Communities and Communalism." *East Asian Pastoral Review* 26, nos. 3–4 (1989): 294–310.

Plagens, Peter. "Violence in Our Culture." *Newsweek* (1 April 1991): 46–49; 51–52.

Poster, Mark. ed. *Jean Baudrillard: Selected Writings*. Stanford, Calif.: Stanford University Press, 1988.

Postman, Neil. "Engaging Students in the Great Conversation." *Phi Delta Kappan* (January 1983): 311–16.

———. *Amusing Ourselves to Death: Public Discourse in the Age of Show Business*. New York: Viking Penguin, 1985.

———. *Teaching as a Conserving Activity*. New York: Delta, 1979. New York: Viking Penguin, 1985.

Power, David. "Liturgy and Culture." *East Asian Pastoral Review* 21, no. 4 (1984): 348–60.

Rapping, Elayne. "Girls Just Wanna Have Fun." *The Nation* (27 August/ 3 September 1990): 206–9.

Reif, Rita. "Antiques: Toys That Go Beyond." *New York Times* (2 March 1986): H26.

"Rising Brutality Complaints Raise Questions about New York Police." *New York Times* (6 May 1985): A1, B5.

Romano, Carlin. "The Grisly Truth about Bare Facts." In R. K. Manoff and Michael Schudson, eds., *Reading the News*. New York: Pantheon Books, 1987.

Rosenthal, Peggy. *Words and Values: Some Leading Words and Where They Lead Us*. New York: Oxford University Press, 1984.

Sachs, William L. "Willimon's Project: Does It Make Sense?" *Christian Century* 106, no. 13 (19 April 1989): 412–14.

Sale, Kirkpatrick "The Trouble with Earth Day." *The Nation* (30 April 1990): 594–98.

Sanders, Thomas. "The Paulo Freire Method." American Universities Field Staff Reports, West Coast South America Series 15, no. 1. Hanover, N.H., 1968.

Schiller, Herbert I. *Culture Inc.: The Corporate Takeover of Public Expression.* New York: Oxford, 1989.

Schiro, Anne-Marie. "Play-Cosmetics for Children: Dissenting Voices Are Heard." *New York Times* (21 February 1981): 13.

Schropp, Mary Lou, ed. *Platform for Action: The Electronic Media, Popular Culture and Family Values.* New York: United States Catholic Conference, Department of Communication, 1985.

Schudson, Michael. "The New Validation of Popular Culture: Sense and Sentimentality in Academia." *Critical Studies in Mass Communication* 4, no. 1 (March 1987): 51–68.

Shaffer, Peter. *Equus.* New York: Avon Books, 1974.

Sheehan, Helena. *Irish Television Drama: A Society and Its Stories.* Dublin: Radio Telefis Eireann, 1987.

Simpson, Craig. "The Violence of War Toys." *The Non-violent Activist* (November–December 1985): 3–6.

Starhawk. *Dreaming the Dark: Magic, Sex, and Politics.* Boston: Beacon Press, 1982.

Steiner, George. *Language and Silence.* New York: Atheneum Books, 1967.

Stevenson, Richard W. "The Selling of Toy 'Concepts.'" *New York Times* (14 December 1985): 33.

Strinati, Dominic. *An Introduction to Theories of Popular Culture.* London and New York: Routledge, 1996.

Surlis, Paul. "The Relation between Social Justice and Inculturation in the Papal Magisterium." In A. A. Roest Crollius, ed., *Creative Inculturation and the Unity of Faith,* Working Papers on Living Faith and Cultures 8. Rome: Gregorian University, 1987.

Tamke, Susan S. *Make a Joyful Noise unto the Lord: Hymns as a Reflection of Victorian Social Attitudes.* Athens: Ohio University Press, 1978.

Tuchman, Barbara. *A Distant Mirror: The Calamitous Fourteenth Century.* New York: Ballantine Books, 1987.

Warren, Michael. "The Worshiping Assembly: Possible Zone of Contestation." *Worship* 63, no. 1 (1989): 2–16.

———. "Cultural Coding in the Young: The On-going Dilemma." *Listening* 25, no. 1 (Winter 1990): 47–60.

———. *Faith, Culture, and the Worshiping Community.* Washington, D.C.: Pastoral Press, 1993.

———. "The Material Conditions of Our Seeing and Perceiving." *New Theology Review* 7, no. 2 (May 1994): 37–59.

————. *Youth, Gospel, Liberation.* New York: Don Bosco Multimedia, 1994.

————. "Judging the Electronic Communications Media." *The Living Light* 31, no. 2 (Winter 1994–95): 54–64.

————. "Life Structure or the Material Conditions of Living: An Ecclesial Task." *New Theology Review* 8, no. 4 (1995): 26–47.

White, Robert A. "Mass Communication and Culture: Transition to a New Paradigm." *Journal of Communication* 33, no. 3 (1983): 279–301.

Whiteside, Thomas. "Onward and Upward with the Arts: Cable — I, II, III." *New Yorker* (20, 27 May, 3 June 1985).

Williams, Raymond. *The Long Revolution.* New York: Columbia University Press, 1961.

————. *The Country and the City.* New York: Oxford University Press, 1973.

————. *Television, Technology and Cultural Form.* New York: Schocken Books, 1975.

————. *Keywords: A Vocabulary of Culture and Society.* New York: Oxford University Press, 1977.

————. *Marxism and Literature.* New York: Oxford University Press, 1977.

————. "Means of Communication as Means of Production." In *Problems in Materialism and Culture.* London and New York: Verso, 1980.

————. *The Sociology of Culture.* New York: Schocken Books, 1982.

————. *Culture and Society 1780–1950.* New York: Columbia University Press, 1983.

————. *The Year 2000.* New York: Pantheon Books, 1983.

————. *Resources of Hope.* London and New York: Verso, 1989.

————, ed. *Contact: Human Communication and Its History.* London: Thames and Hudson, 1981.

Willis, Paul, and Philip Corrigan. "Orders of Experience: The Differences of Working Class Cultural Forms." *Social Text* 7 (1983): 85–103.

Winn, Marie. *The Plug-in Drug: Television, Children, and the Family.* New York: Bantam Books, 1978.

————. *Unplugging the Plug-in Drug.* New York: Viking Penguin, 1987.

Winter, Gibson. *Liberating Creation: Foundations of Religious Social Ethics.* New York: Crossroad, 1981.

Young, Michael F. D. "An Approach to the Study of Curricula as Socially Organized Knowledge." In M. F. D. Young, ed., *Knowledge and Control.* London: Collier-Macmillan, 1971.

# INDEX

action. *See* cultural agency
adolescents. *See* young people
advertising
  consumerism and, 28, 107
  control of young people's
    imaginations by, 9–10
  feminists on, 92
  mimesis and, 134–35
agency. *See* cultural agency
analogies, 159–61
Anderson, Warren M., 163–64
Apple, Michael, 68–69, 76n.6,
  76n.14
Aronowitz, Stanley, 71–72, 73,
  80
attention, 24–25
Augustine, St., 136

Bagdikian, Ben, 25
Barnet, Richard, 168n.8
Baudrillard, Jean, 171–76, 177,
  179, 181, 191, 194n.4,
  194n.10, 194–95n.14,
  195n.19
Baum, Gregory, 33n.9, 54, 186–
  87, 188, 191, 193–94n.1
Beckett, Samuel, 127
Bellah, Robert N., 74, 78n.26,
  79n.27, 87
Benjamin, Walter, 119n.26
Berrigan, Daniel, 159–60
Bhopal, India, 163
Bloom, Allan, 77n.13
Boff, Leonardo, 61n.25, 121n.35

Borges, Jorge Luis, 172
Bourdieu, Pierre, 74–75, 79n.30,
  79n.31, 194n. 8
boycotts, 5
Bush, George, 142

capitalism, 28, 44, 180
Carlsson-Paige, Nancy, 120n.30
censorship, 5–6, 119n.26
children. *See* young people
*Christifideles Laici,* 113–14
Christmas, 158
churches, 10, 51–54. *See also*
  religion; Roman Catholic
  Church
civil rights movement, 55
competition, 31
Congregation for the Doctrine of
  the Faith, 121n.37
conscientious objection, 77n.12
consciousness, 82–85, 117n.5,
  182
consumerism
  advertising and, 28, 107
  hegemony and, 182
  history of, 180–81
  religion and, 26, 30
  young people and, 62–64
consumer-protection rules, 6
consumption. *See* consumerism;
  cultural consumption
contexts, 138–40, 157
corporations, 25, 90–91
Corrigan, Philip, 185, 187